Are You Happy?

ALSO BY EMILY FOX GORDON

Mockingbird Years:
A Life In and Out of Therapy

Are You Happy?

A Childhood Remembered

EMILY FOX GORDON

RIVERHEAD BOOKS

a member of Penguin Group (USA) Inc.

New York

2006

RIVERHEAD BOOKS
Published by the Penguin Group
Penguin Group (USA) Inc., 375 Hudson Street, New York, New York 10014, USA • Penguin
Group (Canada), 90 Eglinton Avenue East, Suite 700, Toronto, Ontario M4P 2Y3, Canada
(a division of Pearson Penguin Canada Inc.) • Penguin Books Ltd, 80 Strand, London
WC2R 0RL, England • Penguin Ireland, 25 St Stephen's Green, Dublin 2, Ireland (a division
of Penguin Books Ltd) • Penguin Group (Australia), 250 Camberwell Road, Camberwell,
Victoria 3124, Australia (a division of Pearson Australia Group Pty Ltd) • Penguin Books
India Pvt Ltd, 11 Community Centre, Panchsheel Park, New Delhi—110 017, India •
Penguin Group (NZ), Cnr Airborne and Rosedale Roads, Albany, Auckland 1310, New
Zealand (a division of Pearson New Zealand Ltd) • Penguin Books (South Africa) (Pty) Ltd,
24 Sturdee Avenue, Rosebank, Johannesburg 2196, South Africa

Penguin Books Ltd, Registered Offices:
80 Strand, London WC2R 0RL, England

This memoir includes material from the essays "Faculty Brat" and "Are You Happy?" published
in *Boulevard,* Spring 1995 (vol. 10, nos. 1–2), and Spring 2001 (vol. 16, no. 3), respectively.

Library of Congress Cataloging-in-Publication Data
Gordon, Emily Fox, date.
Are you happy?: a childhood remembered / Emily Fox Gordon.
p.   cm.
ISBN 1-59448-904-1
1. Gordon, Emily Fox, date—Childhood and youth.   2. Children of teachers—United
States—Biography.   3. Williams College.   I. Title.
LA2317.G62G67   2006   2005044410
974.4'1—dc22
[B]

Printed in the United States of America
1   3   5   7   9   10   8   6   4   2

BOOK DESIGN BY AMANDA DEWEY

While the author has made every effort to provide accurate telephone numbers and Internet
addresses at the time of publication, neither the publisher nor the author assumes any responsibility for errors, or for changes that occur after publication. Further, the publisher does not
have any control over and does not assume any responsibility for author or third-party websites
or their content.

Some names and identifying characteristics have been changed to protect the privacy of the in-
dividuals involved.

For Andy and Katy

Contents

College Place

The happiness of childhood is existential, not psychological. Adults forget this, probably because of envy.

By all rights I should have been unhappy, or at least I should have been after the age of seven. Before that time I was a charming, lively child, a promising early reader, my mother's favorite. After that time I was a shamefaced fatty, an academic failure, a social pariah, a disappointment to my parents. And yet, even at my worst, I was not unhappy. I was sometimes miserable, certainly, but misery is a temporary condition. I cultivated a dumb stoicism—today it might be taken for depression—to get through the worst half hour of teasing at recess. When I was sent to after-school study hall, as I regularly was, I waited until the monitor's back was turned, ducked out the ground-floor window, and ran away into the woods. I felt free there, and after a few minutes spent wandering in circles and mumbling to myself, I was happy once again.

I look back at those times, even the painful ones, with longing. How lucky I was, even in my misery, and how unlucky children are today! It seems terrible to me that they have so little freedom, so little privacy, so few means of escape. Helpful adults hover, activities and appointments are arranged for every extracurricular hour. There is no external escape, no woods to wander off into, only the closed universe of video games. And when adults have colonized a child's mind with drugs that alter personality, there is no internal escape, either.

When I was small I was wildly, unconditionally happy. No child stays that way forever, but even so I managed to keep much of my happiness for years. Feelings of gladness and sadness continued to run through me in discrete layers, like currents in a river. I was eleven or twelve before I reached the stage when feelings become soluble in mood.

Do children still fall from innocence? I know I did. I fell in two stages. The first fall was an automatic consequence of having reached the age of reason, and it coincided with a change in the way my memory recorded experience. Before seven, my memories are flashes against a backdrop of insensible darkness. After seven they become less vivid and more continuous. They form a narrative chain, broken in places, that stretches to the present day. At this age, I began to understand my life as a story, and developed the odd habit of telling myself that story even as I was living my life.

The second fall was a fall from grace. When I turned twelve I committed a willful moral error that marked the end of my childhood. I had come to believe that I was unhappy— I could see myself from the outside by now, and knew that I looked that way. For the first time, I had been given a taste of the approval of my classmates, and I took that thrill to be the happiness I lacked. In an effort to get more of it, I told a new kind of story—a deliberate lie. I was caught, and tenderly offered an absolution that I could not accept. At the very moment it was extended to me I realized what my happiness had been, and knew it was lost to me forever.

—

I was born in 1948 and spent my early childhood on College Place in Williamstown, Massachusetts. My father was a professor of economics, one of those academics who would later influence the making of political and economic policy in Washington. He grew up in South Philadelphia and was one of the first Jews to teach at Williams. My mother was a faculty wife, a woman with many talents and graces. Her background was midwestern and Presbyterian. Both of my parents were quick and irreverent and full of shining promise. At Williams they were at the center of a lively group of economics and political science faculty, combative young intellectuals who rode the secularizing, liberalizing wave of change in American life that would crest as the fifties became the sixties.

My younger brother Andy and I were born fifteen months apart, and when we were small, we were inseparable. Our older sister Katy had been raised more conventionally, but by the time Andy and I came along our parents were absorbed in their interlocked ambitions and far from vigilant. It never occurred to either of them to worry about us as we wandered around this gentle, fostering town ringed by the shadowy Berkshires. The elms stood guard over us; the local dogs greeted us; even the telephone operator knew us by name.

We had the run of the town and traipsed freely through backyards and gardens. Occasionally a faculty wife, the mother of some child we knew, would emerge from her kitchen to assure herself of our well-being—there was a kind of communal attitude toward child rearing in the Williamstown of my youth—but after a brief interrogation we were allowed to go on our way. We rambled down to the swampy woods beyond the athletic fields, where we rolled up our pants legs and waded ankle-deep through warm mud, hunting for frogs. We raced around the plazas and quadrangles of the Williams campus on our bikes, jousting with sticks. We skittered through the stacks of the college library, which were dim and cool and smelled of fungus. Often we had our dog James in tow. (What college library these days would allow two small children and a German shepherd to wander around unsupervised?) We liked to bring him into college buildings because the polished linoleum floors unnerved him. He trotted along gamely until the realization that he was getting no traction with his claws overcame him. Then he collapsed, his legs splaying out beneath him and his eyes rolling in panicky shame. Andy and I took him by the collar and dragged him past the reference librarian's desk and out the door. Once on the grass, he shook himself thoroughly and sprinted across Library Hill toward home.

I remember that librarian quite clearly. I can see her standing at the card catalog, turning to peer at us sharply over her shoulder. She was a trim, mannish, straight-backed woman with closely croppped hair, a former WAC who wore a daily uniform of khaki slacks and crisp white shirt. A lesbian, I realize now. In Williamstown she was one of those people who defied categorization and were filed, in people's minds, under the heading of "local character" or "fixture." We saw her pedal by our house every morning on her Schwinn, her lunch box lashed to the back wheel. To Andy and me, she was simply an adult and, like every adult (except our mother), either a means or an impediment to the realization of our plans. Now I find myself wondering: What could her life have been like in Williamstown, in 1953?

—

Our first house on College Place was directly opposite the library. I looked out my bedroom window at the names carved in marble above the high windows of the reading room—OVID, HORACE, PLATO, EUCLID—and felt a kind of bottomless awe. I knew nothing about these historical figures, only that the contemplation of their names, etched in stone, gave me a thrilling sense of the reach of time, as if I were looking down an endlessly regressing line of colonnades. When my father sat in his study correcting blue books (in his Harvard chair, emblazoned in gold paint with the motto VERITAS), I took him to be in direct communication with ARISTOTLE and PLATO. In reality, his knowledge of the ancients was not much deeper than my own. His god was a modern one, John Maynard Keynes.

No child could have been more primitively credulous than I. Growing up on a college campus, surrounded by books and by architecture that made reference to a vague and glorious history, I assumed that my parents and their friends were the recipients of all the wisdom of the past. As evidence for my intuition I had only the unchanging peace of our small academic enclave, the shade of maples and elms, the echoing hush of the library reading room, the glow of red brick in late afternoon sun. When I was a child, these things were enough to make me believe that we were living in an Arcadia at the end of time.

The decay of this illusion was the story of my childhood, perhaps the story of my life. Like all children, I was an emotional conservative, even—or especially—in the face of my parents' confident liberalism. Only when my family was preparing to leave Williamstown in 1960 did I begin to understand that my parents were representatives of the future, not the past. Only when I became an adult did I realize that the soil in which my life had been planted was not the deep loam I had always taken it to be, but a thin layer of dry stuff any strong wind could blow away.

If certain intractable problems remained in the world, my father and his colleagues could be depended upon to haul them up into the light of reason. That was what I understood him to be doing when he spent afternoons in his study with his friend and fellow economist Emile Despres. Emile was ungainly and intensely cerebral, so tall he folded himself in thirds to sit down. He couldn't have been much older than forty at the time, but his long balding head and the gravity of his bearing made him seem sixty. He treated Andy and me with an abstracted tenderness; only when we placed ourselves directly in his path did he notice us. "Ah," he would say, "children," as if pleased to be reminded that such a category existed, and he would bend down from his precipitous height to bestow a ceremonial pat on each of our heads.

We were forbidden to disturb my father and Emile while they were "discussing" in my father's study, but we liked to linger outside the door. Our nostrils drew in vagrant shreds of the tobacco miasma that swirled in that room: my father smoked a pipe and Emile was never without a cigarette. We heard our father's voice, always dominant, and Emile's questioning or corroborating hums and murmurs. When he spoke, Andy and I stifled our giggles; his voice was abnormally deep and cracked like an adolescent's. His laugh was even stranger, a series of desperate gasping wheezes, each followed by a small gulping sob, as though whatever had amused him had also caused him sorrow. My father was a big impressive man with a big powerful mind, but I think he considered Emile his intellectual superior. He treated him with deference and made a joke of calling him "Boss." Later I learned that James Finney Baxter, the president of the college, referred to my father and Emile as "those two Jews."

While my father and Emile were thinking their way through the problems of late modernity, my mother and her fellow faculty wives were busy reforming local politics and perfecting everyday life. In the Williamstown of those days, "faculty wife" was more than a descriptive designation; it was a calling, and implied membership in a society of like-minded and often rivalrous women. Faculty wives baked their own bread, grew their own produce in backyard gardens during the short Berkshire summers, sent their children to school with wholesome lunches packed in brown paper bags. They understood the importance of vitamins and "roughage." They drank wine with dinner. They were the first generation to follow the dictates of Spock. In defiance of the views of their own mothers, they breast-fed their babies, chain-smoking all the while. These children were raised according to psychologically enlightened principles, and many were pronounced gifted.

Faculty wives manned the pricing tables at the local Women Exchange, which donated its profits to the Visiting Nurse Association. They sold baked goods to further worthy causes. They worked to improve the schools, to fluoridate the water (some local people believed fluoridation to be a Communist plot), and to field Democratic candidates to run for local office. They wrote letters to the *Berkshire Eagle* and the *North Adams Transcript,* deploring hazing practices in the fraternities.

My mother was one of these women. For a while she served as president of the local chapter of the League of Women Voters. I remember that, because she was in place as president when I failed to win a prize at the League's Halloween pageant, even though the costume she had made for me that year was a spectacular octopus rig with a bulbous papier-mâché head and eight battleship-gray tentacles stuffed with cotton and weighted with pebbles. I swaggered across the stage at the Williamstown grange in that costume to much applause, swinging my many arms like coshes. But in the end I was disqualified, due to what my mother called a "conflict of interest." As I recall, my mother lasted only one term as League president. She was popular among the wives, but her civic engagement was perfunctory; she was too much an ironist to be an activist. By the time I began elementary school, she had drifted away from the political end of things and had taken over as avatar of the aesthetic wing of faculty wife society.

Many of the wives had artistic inclinations. They spent their days at the kiln or the canvas or the loom or the typewriter. A few were seriously ambitious. Sascha Dillard, an abstract painter and a problem drinker, rented a railroad apartment on Spring Street and used it as a studio. Anna Winslow converted her garage to a metalworking studio. Andy and I stood on tiptoe at the side window to get a look at her, hooded and goggled, standing in the darkness in a corona of sparks.

My mother viewed these women with a certain wry skepticism, which I picked up and imitated. She was delighted, for example, when Sascha's husband, an anthropology professor, sabotaged the opening of his wife's show by affixing a $19.95

price tag to her biggest and splashiest canvas. Although she was regarded as a kind of Renaissance woman among the wives—she wrote poetry and short stories, sketched and painted in watercolors, played the piano—my mother was no more capable of passion for art than for politics. To throw oneself unreservedly into anything was to risk appearing ridiculous. This included sex; my mother made savage fun of a few amateur vamps among the wives.

She disarmed her rivals by presenting her accomplishments as amateur dabblings. It was *sprezzatura,* really, and she rightly expected the other wives to admire her all the more for it. This attitude was one of a number of notions I've inherited from her, all of which have turned out to be maladaptive. Some others were: Don't be tiresome. Don't wear out your welcome. Let them come to you. Leave them laughing.

The domestic arts were the only arena in which she felt free to compete without inhibition. She was a fairly casual housekeeper—most faculty wives were; Williamstown in the fifties was not Betty Friedan's suburbia—but a prolific seamstress and an inspired cook. She reduced beef bones to a gelatinous essence in a stockpot on a back burner of the stove, ran poached chicken livers through a meat grinder for pâté, taught herself to master the arts of meringue and puff pastry. Somehow, she got her hands on limes and pineapples in the dead of Berkshire winters; she lobbied the Brundage brothers, who ran the local A&P, to supply her with endives and escarole. She garnished her dinner party plates with sprigs of watercress she found growing wild on the banks of the Green River (until a dinner party guest took her aside and warned her that the river was polluted with sewage).

Her standards were exacting, even for everyday meals. During the two weeks in August when she judged corn on the cob to be fit for human consumption, she set two pots of water boiling on the back of the stove in the late afternoon, piled Andy and me into our boxy green Plymouth station wagon, and drove out Main Street in the direction of North Adams. We turned right before the old A&P and followed a dirt road to Tom Fowler's farm. His hermit's shack sat like a dinghy in a sea of high corn, and Tom himself was always waiting out front for us, as though he understood the urgency of our mission. One of his front teeth had been broken in two and home-repaired with a line of dark epoxy. "Dozen?" he asked. My mother nodded and he dove into his fields, emerging five minutes later with a paper bag packed tight with thirteen silk-tufted ears, which he settled into my mother's outstretched arms like a love offering. I don't remember that she paid, though I suppose she must have. (Some years later, Tom Fowler surprised us by taking a bride, a managing woman who established a sideline in strawberry jam and corncob dolls.) We drove directly home, shucked the corn, and plunged it into the boiling water. Seven minutes later we were seated at the table. Whatever else my mother served for dinner on Tom Fowler nights was superfluous; the essentials were corn, butter, salt, hands, teeth. I still eat corn on the cob greedily, in and out of season. But it no longer tastes like joy and I no longer need to be stopped before I make myself sick.

After dinner there were still two hours left to spend loping up and down Library Hill with a loose aggregation of fellow faculty brats. We played hide-and-seek on those summer evenings, or captured fireflies in Mason jars with ventilated lids, until the long winking twilight was doused by darkness and we were called into the house for bed.

———

Most of the faculty wives I knew were kind to me. When I began to have my troubles, a few took me aside and offered the kind of encouragement that can feed a lonely child for years, though at the time I felt obliged to stare at my shoes and shrug away the hand on my shoulder. Even so, I never doubted that my mother was superior to them all. Compared to her, the political wives were flat-footed in their earnestness, the artistic wives affected and self-important. Nobody was as effortlessly good at so many things as my mother; nobody had her self-deprecating light touch, nobody's judgments were so modest and yet so unassailable.

I learned later that there were whisperings among some of the wives about the latitude my mother allowed Andy and me. Perhaps we were indeed neglected, but we never for a moment felt it. She charmed us, kept us in a state of perpetual delight. Life was full of treats and surprises and much-anticipated pleasures. For our birthdays she baked a lamb cake, which she frosted with vanilla icing, tinting a little of it pink, for use on the tip of the lamb's nose and the insides of its ears, and studded with curls of coconut (she cracked it open with a screwdriver and a hammer, decanted the liquid, cut the meat from the shell, shaved and toasted it). She read to us on demand and was often willing to sit at the piano banging out "Casey Jones" and "Clementine" and other tiresome favorites from the *Fireside Book of Folk Songs* while I sat next to her on the embroidered bench, warbling.

Unlike the other mothers we knew, she was a partisan of childhood, with a special appreciation for its freedoms and delights. She remembered her own vividly and told us stories about how she spent hours in the Winnetka woods, arranging acorn teacups on beds of moss for the fairies. Sometimes you can catch one for an instant in the corner of your eye, she told us—a flash, a glittering flutter.

Instead of opposing childhood, as those other mothers sometimes seemed to do, she ushered Andy and me into ours and encouraged us to explore it. At first we stayed within the boundaries of College Place, herded away from the street by James, who was an anxious nursemaid of a dog. But as we grew older and our investigations took us farther afield, we felt that we went with her blessing.

She was quite lovely when she was young, small-boned and deep-bosomed, with a delicate turned-up nose and a head of anarchically wavy brown hair that she tried to control with bobby pins. "Hair-colored hair," she called it. She loved pretty clothes, and made many of her own, but for everyday she dressed in pants and lace-up boots and a short quilted jacket: in some early snapshots taken from a distance, she looks a little like a Chinese peasant. She was a bit of a flirt, an admirer of Dorothy Parker, an accomplished hostess, a witty anecdotalist. Her charm had to do with the contrast between her air of aloof sensitivity and her unexpectedly pungent sense of humor.

An example: she liked to tell a story about a young poet she knew in college. One day she and this young man (where was my father in this picture?) went walking through a new-fallen snow, the first of the season. The beauty of the scene sent the poet into ecstasies: "How pristine! How perfect!" "Yeah," my mother quoted herself as having replied—lowering her voice to a growl to deliver the line—"just like a goddamn Christmas card." Guests at our table never failed to burst into startled laughter. Andy and I laughed, too, uproariously, no matter how many times we heard this story. We laughed at all my mother's anecdotes, even those we were unequipped to understand. What could we have made, for instance, of our mother's dinner party version of the old Mother Goose rhyme:

> There was an old woman who lived in a shoe.
> She had so many children she didn't know what to
>   do—
> Obviously.

or this revision of Robert Burns:

> The best-planned lays o' mice an' men gang aft agley.

I think we laughed from a kind of relief. We took her sense of humor to be the true north of her personality. There was something reassuring about the way she turned her wit on herself, banishing for the moment whatever it was in her that sometimes seemed a little fey and haunted.

———

When I say that I was happy, I don't mean I was well-adjusted or that I was raised according to principles of psychological hygiene. My life was not untroubled, even when I was very small. For one thing, my father was perpetually erupting in irritation at me. I was sloppy, wasteful, clumsy, forgetful, impulsive. I slammed doors, left my clothes in heaps on the floor, dribbled food onto my shirt and lap, needed reminding to put the cap back on the toothpaste. I have an early memory of falling downstairs and looking up to see him standing over me, hands on his hips, shaking his head deploringly. "I don't know whether to laugh or cry at you, Emily," he said, and walked away. That still stings in memory. Even so, I managed mostly to ignore him. I was almost stupidly resilient, and in the end my father simply wasn't very important. My mother occupied the greater part of the firmament of my existence; he was a minor figure, an irascible North Wind puffing at me from a far corner of the celestial map.

When I say I was happy, I mean that all my receptors were attuned to the world, that I felt things freshly and keenly, that my mind received impressions so indelibly that memories from this period stay true in my memory, like colored stones submerged in water. I rose out of bed every day full of anticipatory joy, in such a hurry to be up and exploring that I often forgot to brush my teeth or put my clothes on right side out.

Part of what made me happy was the sense that my life had purpose. The world was a treasure hunt designed for Andy and me, and my job was to take the lead in finding what had been left for us to discover. (In pictures of the two of us from this period, I'm very much the older sister, holding Andy's hand tightly and draping a proprietary arm around his shoulder.) Who was the great designer? God. Growing up in an agnostic family, I was nevertheless a believer, with a worked-out theology: God made the world and had since retired to a realm of unchanging forms, leaving my mother in charge.

Or at least I was a half believer, and one of the things I half believed was that my mother was present even when she was absent, that in some attentuated form she moved ahead of Andy and me as we penetrated farther into unexplored woods and meadows. Sometimes I believed that the world *was* her mind. I never felt that our rambles took us away from her; on the contrary, the farther we wandered, the closer to her I felt we were approaching.

Andy and me and my mother: that was the magic circle. My father and sister lived outside it. (She tells me now that she envied Andy and me our closeness to each other and to our mother.) James was one of us too, of course. He appears in many photographs in his capacity as canine governess, leaning in to lick our shoulders as Andy and I sit together in the bathtub, or flanking us protectively as we loll, toddler and infant, in the long grass of Library Hill. The circle broke when we were six and seven and began to do our wandering apart as well as together. Our mother's presence was no longer with us when we rambled separately. That was when she began her long, slow retreat.

—

We moved from Williamstown to New York in 1960, when I was twelve, and then almost immediately to Washington, D.C. My history as a teenager was a checkered one, involving continued school failure and much psychotherapy. I was a mildly delinquent adolescent, more sullen than actively defiant. (Today the girl I was then would be described as "oppositional.") I was expelled from boarding school, failed to graduate from the Washington high school I was sent to next, and was too preoccupied with a boyfriend to bother with applying to colleges. Instead, my parents enrolled me in the Austen Riggs Center, an expensive mental hospital in Stockbridge, Massachusetts, not far from Williamstown, where my father's government insurance policy covered the fees. As an adolescent I was in thrall to the romance of mental illness, and my parents' decision to institutionalize me represented the realization of a long-cherished fantasy.

The three years I spent there were years I should have spent in college, but I suppose that Riggs was itself a kind of education, if only in the many varieties of boredom. I moved on to New York, worked at low-paying jobs, studied intermittently, struggled with poverty and my own disorganization. When I was twenty-four I married a young assistant professor of philosophy, and in the years after that I became a kind of faculty wife myself, though not quite in the spirit of my mother and her contemporaries. I drank a lot, moderated my drinking, enrolled as a student in the university where my husband taught, completed a B.A. and a master's degree in English, and began to try my hand at writing.

My daughter was born in 1982. A decade later my husband was recruited by Rice University and we moved to Houston. I began to publish essays in literary quarterlies, and in 2000 I published a memoir about the ways in which psychotherapy had influenced my life. The achievement would have made my mother proud: she had always predicted a literary destiny for me. It would have made her wretched too, because in my book I wrote openly about her alcoholism.

I'm fifty-six now. My life has turned out, in a small and belated but undeniable way, to be a success. After thirty-two years, my marriage is strong and close. My daughter, herself married now, has grown up to be an estimable person.

Both my parents have been dead for many years. My father died of a heart attack following surgery to repair the damage caused by six months of pancreatitis. He was not quite sixty and still following out the trajectory of a career that began when he left Williams to go to work full-time for the Ford Foundation. From New York he was summoned to serve on Kennedy's Council of Economic Advisers and went on to be named budget director under Johnson. At the start of the Nixon administration he became president of the Brookings Institution. His portrait—an eerily accurate likeness done from a photograph—still hangs in a conference room there.

Late on the night of his death his surgeon and family doctor walked together from the hospital to break the news to my mother. It was twenty minutes from the George Washington University Hospital to my parents' brownstone in the embassy district. The doctors could have driven, but they walked, I suppose, to mark the occasion of the death of an important man and as a gesture of respect for my mother, who was in a fragile condition after my father's long illness. I often think about their solemn progress through empty city streets on that hot night in early July; I like to picture the doctors in their shirtsleeves, crossing the P Street bridge under high haloed streetlamps.

My mother survived my father for twenty-two years. She had always hated Washington, and after his death she moved back to Williamstown to a summerhouse she and my father had acquired and renovated some years earlier. When the winters got to be too much, she moved into a recently built condominium development within a stone's throw of what used to be Tom Fowler's cornfields. She lived there for ten or twelve years in the company of a yellow Lab, designing and executing what she called "needlepoint tapestries" and writing a witty weekly column for the *Berkshire Eagle*. For a while she was active in the governing association of the condominium, but that enthusiasm withered away. Mostly she drank. She turned away from friends and took several gin-related falls.

Fearing for her safety, Andy and Katy persuaded her to move to the Steeples in Lenox, one of those enlightened "levels-of-care" institutions where elderly people live in their own apartments for as long as possible and move to a ward facility only if they become incapacitated. It was a cushy, expensive place: my sister described the decor as "Martha Stewart Microwave Colonial." Several of my mother's faculty wife friends from Williamstown were living there, but as it turned out, Katy and Andy were wrong in assuming she'd enjoy their proximity; instead she viewed them as witnesses to her disgrace.

The conventional wisdom about my mother's alcoholism was that it began after my father's death. I know it started much earlier, but I really can't establish the time of its onset. Was she drinking hard in the early Washington years? Probably. In New York? Possibly. In Williamstown? Conceivably, but not (I insist) before I was seven. At any rate, the deep shame she felt about her drinking had made her incapable of intimacy long before she moved to the Steeples. In the afternoons she was wan, distracted, formal. In the evenings her face was wreathed in rueful smiles; she waved a cigarette, repeated familiar stories. She was warm and animated, but a question would throw her off her anecdotal rails, leave her silent and baffled for a moment. She was really no more accessible drunk than sober. By the time she moved to the Steeples, she could no longer be reached from the outside.

Both my siblings felt alienated from my mother, but they were conscientiously attentive. Andy lived nearby and dropped by to check on her every day. Katy, who lived in Boston, called her regularly and consulted with her doctors. Twice she confronted my mother about her drinking. I stayed far away in Houston, and on the few occasions when I did visit, I took care to get just as drunk as she did. My justification for my neglect was that of the three of us children I had suffered worst at the hands of our parents. My siblings seemed to buy this.

I can't blame my mother for disliking the Steeples. How painful it must have been for her, whose hair was still hair-colored (nobody believed it was natural, but it was) and whose wit and eye for beauty were still largely intact, to be trapped without a driver's license among these creeping elders. I visited her there twice, both times at my sister's urging. Residents were required to show up for at least one meal a day, and after a protracted cocktail hour I accompanied her to the dining room one night. I surveyed the residents grouped around tables, walkers parked within easy reach, eating their small, sad, aggressively garnished dinners. No corner-cutting here: that was the message. See the chandeliers (turned up to blazing brightness for the sake of failing eyes)? See the nonskid strips on the carpet? See the floor-length drapes? See the crystal water glasses, the crushed ice, the elaborately folded linen napkins, the real flowers on every table? See the radish roses? My mother examined her plate, first with suspicion and finally with disgust, which she registered by raising one corner of her upper lip in a delicate sneer.

Some months after that visit, my mother passed out in her apartment and dropped a lit cigarette on the carpet, which cut a burn-channel through the nap all the way to the wall. The management threatened eviction, but my sister managed to persuade them to allow her a chance to dry out at the Brattleboro Retreat. After her return, she managed to keep her intake down to manageable levels for a year or so, but when I called her, as always, at Katy's urging, I could tell by her tone of muzzy hauteur that she had been drinking heavily. I called again a few days later, earlier in the evening, and caught her in a flood of tears. "I *hate* it here," she sobbed, and suddenly she was eighteen again, a young girl bursting with an uncontainable sorrow. It was as if she had opened a vein and was spilling fresh blood. My heart, which had been hardened against her for years, briefly softened. As I registered this I felt a momentary flush of self-satisfaction. At last I'm *feeling* something for her, I thought, and resolved to call her the next morning. When I did, she seemed to have no memory of her tears or, for that matter, our conversation. She sounded perky, but I could hear the strain of the effort, and also a underlying befuddlement. Her smoker's cough had worsened. "Lovely to talk to you, Em," she said, after a conversation that couldn't have lasted more than two minutes. "Now I must pull up my socks and get to work on my Eaglet." That was what she called her newspaper column, which by then had made her a minor local celebrity.

A year or so after that, she underwent hip replacement surgery. My sister and brother did their stints at her bedside, and when it was clear that she was not recovering normally, they reminded me of my duty. I flew from Houston and spent a week with my mother. Mostly I sat in silence, listening to her moan and mutter. Early on, I did my best to coax her to eat, even tried to hand-feed her, but when she retracted her lip in the familiar cat sneer, I gave up in discouragement. (My sister tells me that once, in response to a nurse's question about what she would like to eat, my mother smiled and whispered, "I want a sidereal sandwich." Always literary, my mother.) When it was time for her physical therapy—a nurse shifted my mother's legs so that they projected over the side of the bed and then pulled her slowly to her feet—I beat a cowardly retreat out of the room into the hallway.

I've had many years now to reflect on the inadequacy of

my care for my mother in the hospital that week, the oppor-
tunities for rapprochement that I let pass. But I did have the
presence of mind to notice that her hair was so filthy it was
standing on end, and I did think to ask a nurse how to get in
touch with the itinerant hairdresser. On the afternoon of the
last day of my stay, a sausage-plump, pink-faced Polish woman
named Estella arrived at the door of the hospital room,
wheeling a cart loaded with bottles and hoses and a portable
basin. My mother propped herself on her elbows and made a
little crowing noise of welcome. Soon the spartan little hospital room was filled with steam and with the atavistic fragrance
of an old-fashioned hair salon—the modest, inexpensive kind
where women of my mother's age kept standing weekly appointments. Was that Lustre-Creme Shampoo I smelled? If so,
Pittsfield, Massachusetts, must have been one of the last mar-
kets in the world where it was sold.

Estella gave a very thorough shampoo, really a scalp mas-
sage, working up great peaked caps of lather that fell away in
pearly clots. My mother let her neck go slack and groaned
with pleasure, a deep, abandoned noise that caused the nurse
who sat in the corner making chart notes to look up sharply.
I've thought about that sound many times since. It was as if
all the craving, suffering regions of her brain had been
flooded by a warm tide of relief. I could have waited another
five minutes or even another twenty without missing my
plane, but this seemed an auspicious moment to say good-

bye. (Leave them laughing.) I edged over to the side of the bed, kissed my mother on the forehead, and left the room. That was the last time I saw her; the hip mended eventually, but she died two months later of a heart attack.

A week after I returned to Houston, I received a thank-you note from my mother, written from the hospital in a shaky hand on yellow lined paper. Her writing style was quite intact. What a hardwired attribute it was! The self-deprecation and brittle wit, the high contrast between the formality of diction and the pungent—if antique—colloquialisms, and the characteristic Wodehousian allusions were all present. It reads:

Dear Emmy,

It has been such a long time since I settled down to write something (weeks and weeks) that I'm not sure just what the end product will be. But I didn't want another day to go by without writing to thank you for your extraordinary efforts on my behalf these past days. Believe me, my dearest, they were *much* appreciated, particularly since I don't think I ever felt worse than I have recently. You were so upbeat, and [illegible] and had such a talent for smoking a nurse out of deep cover—can't tell you how grateful I am.

Have just returned from an hour's seasonal entertainment. High jinks among the [illegible], breaking a pinata. Mao, my Chinese PT leader, said I could go

after an hour, but then reneged and was condemned
to stay up *another* hour for my sins. I'm not sure I can
handle this PT rap. Anyway, for all your help in keeping a lunatic ancestress as much on the rails as poss.,
all thanks.

Only a reader as thoroughly trained in the subtle grada-
tions of my mother's use of endearments as I could be expected to catch the significance of that "my dearest." It was a
pearl of genuine affection, set deep and off center in the
elaborate filigree of her letter.

—

There's nothing more tiresome than a grown daughter's
brief against her parents. It's become a genre all by itself, and
a stale one. For years I kept my parents' offenses against me
inscribed in my heart. Mostly it was my mother I blamed. In
the unfair way of such things I was inclined to let my father
off the hook, if only because I loved him less.

Once, in an effort to purge myself of my resentments, I
tried the exercise of writing them out, but I gave up after
making a few entries. On the page, these bullet-point regis-
trations look embarrassingly petty. I'm too much my mother's
daughter to risk appearing ridiculous, even for therapeutic

purposes and even (or especially) to myself. But it was never really my mother's actions that I held against her anyway. It was her attitudes: her passivity, her willful fatalism, her arrogant disappointment with life. The first two of these traits I recognize in myself. The last has always baffled me.

With encouragement from therapists, I tried several times to work my anger up to a transformative pitch, but I was never able to achieve a satisfying catharsis. For one thing, I've never quite accepted psychological explanations of my childhood. They don't accord with my sense of having lost an original Eden. For another, even on those occasions when I found my therapists' causal accounts too attractive to resist, I found I simply could not disown my sense of proportion. I knew that my mother was not a bad parent. (My father was, but he lacked aptitude.) She never burned us with cigarettes or abused or abandoned us. In fact, she was much more than adequate; she was inspired. She offered us the gift of what psychologists would call an "enriched early environment." It's a valuable inheritance, if not an easy one to spend.

And she was so sad. I don't feel anger anymore; I'm not sure I ever really did. These days, what I feel when I think about my mother is a diminished thing: a mild, pervasive melancholy with an admixture of puzzlement. I bring to mind an image of the blooming mother of my childhood. Then I picture the mother in the hospital bed in Pittsfield, her face very small, her wasted arms as dark and leathery as a premature baby's. I ask myself, How could the two be the same? In my mind, the connection is severed.

—

When my mother was a year or two older than I am now, she mentioned to me that in idle moments her mind had begun to return—"steal back" was the phrase she used—to the Winnetka of her childhood. Recently, I've developed the same tendency. Sitting at my desk or in the car at a stoplight, or lying in bed waiting for sleep, I steal back to Williamstown. I sweep from one end of the town to the other, following the straight line of Main Street like a low-flying airplane, hovering above the campus, passing over the Haystack Monument and the infirmary and the tennis courts and the woods beyond them. Or I take another angle, starting, for example, above the road to Bennington and cutting a swath over the reach of brushy wilderness we children called "New Inverness." There's no particular emotion connected to these thought-excursions, only a faint sensation of reassurance, like the feeling of running my tongue around the inside of my mouth.

My earliest memories of College Place are quite different. They're single, still snapshots, some of them quite arbitrary: a glimpse of the back of a white clapboard garage, for example, half obscured by a holly bush. They carry the air of that time and place, as if the College Place in my mind had been lying under an unbroken seal for fifty years. What I feel when I summon them is pure and potent nostalgia. It's my old happiness, magically retrieved. I'm tempted to say it's my lost love for my mother that returns to me, but that's not quite right. She's absent from these pictures, or if she's present, it's only parts of her—a tweed shoulder, a section of her cheek—that I can visualize. Even so, in my memory her absence is full of her presence, just as it was when I was small. She infuses everything.

It's true that my happiness was founded on a childish misunderstanding of reality. Many of the circumstances that would later make me unhappy were present in my early life, but of course I was not yet equipped to understand that. I was happy, and my happiness was real. Only in stories can conflict and sadness be registered and recorded, and while I was fascinated by stories when I was small, my life itself had not yet become one. It was not made of incidents, which are susceptible to being linked in a causal chain. Instead it was a succession of moments of radiant apprehension.

The College Place in my mind is absolutely intact and eerily accessible, but only to me. Strictly speaking, these memories are incommunicable. I can't tell a picture; describing isn't telling. What I can tell is a story, and the story I tell over and over is the one everyone knows: the story about how happiness is lost.

Seven-five-four
Emily

I was two, toddling around in the small yard between the back of the house and the lilac bushes, unsupervised except by Dickie Barnes, who was five and lived next door. It was a warm day in late spring or early summer; the grass was long and studded with dandelions.

Dickie and I watched as a bumblebee hovered and lighted on a blossom. He leaned down, took my hand, and used it to pantomime a stroking motion in the air above the bee, which detached itself from the dandelion and flew off a few feet to visit another. Dickie gripped me by the shoulders and frog-marched me a few feet this way, a few that, following the bee on its zigzagging course. We must have made a touching sight, a small child showing the world to one still smaller.

I was deeply charmed by the bee. Poised in the air an inch above the grass, its sketchy landing apparatus drawn up under its smartly banded black and yellow body, it was a thing I longed to touch. So fat! So fuzzy! Dickie, that pedagogue, whispered inducements in my ear. The bee descended into the aureole of a dandelion. I reached out, extended a finger.

The shock has fixed the memory. I retain an indelible image of the springy young grass, the great flat dandelions, my corduroy-clad knees as I squatted to pat the bee. I remember the sky, the leafy lilac bushes, the bay window that looked out from the back of the house, hung with straw-colored hopsacking curtains my mother had run up on her Singer in the attic sewing room. I'd been standing in that window a few minutes earlier when Dickie appeared and beckoned. I remember the sting itself as an explosion of yellow.

This is not my first memory, only the first of my memories that records an incident. Actually, that's not true: there's another one, even earlier. I remember waking from a nap in my crib, finding my loaded diaper lying open next to me on the sheet, thinking, *What's this?* and reaching out—that inquiring finger once again!—to hook a little of the warm stuff and bring it to my mouth.

—

The Williams campus is an uncloistered one, with barnlike old houses distributed randomly among the academic buildings. Many of these have been taken over by the college now. The smaller ones house special programs; the larger have become dorms. But fifty years ago they were faculty dwellings, leased by the college to Williams professors and their families. College Place was a nest of three of these houses, flanked on two sides by college buildings. We lived, in sequence, in two of these, directly next door to one another. If I recall correctly, we paid a monthly rent of $125.

The first was the eccentrically constructed gray house, where Andy and I were born. The second was a stodgy white Victorian with a circular driveway, a front yard that froze over in winter and could be used for skating, a covered side porch that looked out on the annexes of the Williams Inn, and a stand of horse chestnut trees that threw fronded shadows in the afternoon. The gray house and the white house were barely fifty yards apart, but so different from one another that I think of them as separate ecosystems. The gray one was a kind of overgrown rambling cottage with deep, white-painted ornamental eaves. It was set beyond a stand of pines, directly across the street from Fernald Hall, where the economics department kept its offices. My father crossed College Place every morning in his khakis and tweed jacket, briefcase in hand, and returned every afternoon, sometimes with a clutch of blue books to grade.

The kitchen of the gray house was long and rather dark. My mother seated my brother and me at our own small wooden table at the window for our breakfasts and lunches. I have a photograph of Andy and me, three and two respectively, sitting in profile at that table with bowls of oatmeal and glasses of milk before us. It's a tryptich of three snapshots, actually, black-and-white ones, which my mother mounted on olive green matting. This framed series of pictures was one of the things I took from her last apartment when she died five years ago.

In the first frame, Andy and I address our breakfasts, our chins tucked into our chests. In the second the camera has caught us beginning to look up; something has captured our attention. In the third we're exploding in laughter; we've dropped our spoons and thrown our heads back. Someone has said something funny! (We were easily amused.) When I look at these photographs, my eye is drawn past the two children and out the kitchen window to a blowsy, blurred view of elms. Looking at them, I'm reminded that what was recorded here was not only a representative moment, but also a historical one. It was a winter morning, judging by my long-sleeved jersey and Andy's sweater. Someone had said something funny, probably my mother, who knew how to make us laugh. This happened more than fifty years ago and a number of those tall vague trees outside the window have long since been cut down. In the photographs they have the faintly ominous look of an authenticating detail.

Andy was a confectionary little boy, blond, pudgy, solemn in the company of strangers. When my mother took us to the Penney's in the neighboring mill town of North Adams to buy us new socks and overalls, elderly ladies were drawn to him irresistibly. "What a darling child!" they cooed. Andy glared. On one occasion, when he was three years old, some woman utterly forgot herself and tried to hoist him into the air. "Get your grimy paws off me," he said.

Our mother saw Andy and me as near-twins and encouraged our intimacy. When we were very small she trained us to bow together from the waist when we were introduced to adults. Until I turned six and Andy five, we shared not only a bedroom but also a bathtub; I have another series of photographs showing the two of us in the water—laughing again— our mother perched on the rim of the tub, James hovering, his wagging tail a blur. Once a week we took turns standing on a small stool at the kitchen sink to have our hair washed under the tap. I was stoical. Andy wailed.

Together, we invented a pair of fur-bearing monsters that lived in the attic adjoining our room: the angry Attichin and his conciliatory nephew, the Mooshla. We shared, or at least we believed that we had shared, a nightmare in which a mechanical monkey with eyes and teeth that flashed red raced around the walls of our room, making a terrifying grinding noise. With each revolution another monkey was sucked out of the toy box and as they proliferated they spun faster and faster, flashing and grinding until Andy and I—at least I remember it this way—both woke up screaming.

———

I have a clutch of recollections that I find by revisiting a guest bedroom on the second floor of the Barneses' house, a place to retire when play with Dickie and his brother Russell got too rough. It was a narrow corner room with two hypnotic windows at the far end, one looking east and one south, each with its own view. In my imagination I can walk into and through that room right now and look down over the two gardens of my childhood through those portals of memory.

The window in the wall facing east oversaw a communal kitchen garden shared by my mother and two of the other faculty wives who lived on College Place. Andy and I sat in the rows of that garden as infants while my mother knelt and weeded in her straw hat and gloves. Later she allowed us to pull pale new carrots out of the ground, which we wiped on our overalls and ate on the spot, and still later we learned to raid the garden on our own, stripping tiny green beans from the vines and loading our pockets with fruit from the currant bushes. Anthony and Patrick Quinn, the quarrelsome twin sons of the funeral director who lived in a square yellow house below the Barneses' on Southworth Street, a little beyond our academic enclave, got into the garden at least once every August and pelted each other with my mother's tomatoes.

And one summer, when our family hosted three foreign exchange students, an Indian, a Pakistani, and an African, all men in their thirties with faraway wives and children of their own, my mother collaborated with the Indian on an elaborate vegetarian curry that fed the entire economics department and some political scientists as well. Andy and I gathered baskets of eggplant and zucchini from the garden under the Indian student's supervision and my mother spent the day doing her best to follow his exacting directions in the kitchen. The Indian was the one Andy and I liked least: he took a harsh tone with us, and while he seemed to disapprove of nearly everything my mother prepared, he made a pig of himself whenever ice cream was served. We preferred the Pakistani, who used our bedroom to bow to Mecca five times a day. This was a practice that magical thinkers like Andy and I found so appealing that we took it up ourselves for a while after he left. Our favorite was the African, who let us ride on his back and grew teary-eyed when he opened his wallet to show us photographs of his own small sons and daughters.

Through the southern window I look out on a row of tall, symmetrical pines, over the sweep of lawn in front of one of the green-shuttered Williams Inn annexes where I befriended, for one summer, a sad little girl in white gloves who had been sent there to live with a great-aunt while her parents divorced. She and I held a friendship ceremony—in the garage, for some reason—where we exchanged symbolic tokens. She gave me a shamrock charm from her bracelet. I gave her a brick.

Another friend lived in the annex, an elderly woman named Mrs. Thorn. I first encountered her when Andy and I were rocking in the rocking chairs on the wide porch there. For some reason she showed an interest in me and I took up the practice of visiting her apartment. (I was a great one for dropping by.) I have very little memory of those occasions, only the feel of the shiny mahogany banister sliding under my hand as I climbed the stairs, the painted boards of the ceiling above me receding away, teaching me my first lesson in perspective. I remember the wicker love seat in which I sat and a cloisonné jar of peonies somewhere at the end of a long, peaceful room. I remember being given a glass of lemonade and a brownie with a sprinkling of powdered sugar on its crust, and I remember my anxiety about managing without a surface to put them on. I can't seem to bring up an image of my hostess, though I do recall feeling that in her company I was expected to be on my best behavior. Mrs. Thorn was a widow and a southerner. (I wonder now: why were there so many southerners in the Williamstown of my childhood?) She had a sister named Mrs. Rose, or so she told me. She had no children. She kept a stock of shell-shaped chocolates and crystalized ginger. Once she gave me a string of real pearls, the value of which I understood only later.

Beyond the annex I see the street that wound down the hill toward Southworth Street, and beyond that the Williams Inn garden, a real working garden in those days and a place my brother and I haunted at all the stages of our childhood. When we were very small, we hatched a plan to dig a tunnel and construct a train that would carry us back and forth between the bedroom we shared and the inn garden. This was not feasible; we understood that. We pictured the tunnel as originating in the floor of our bedroom, and of course our bedroom was on the second floor. Needless to say, we had no idea how to build a train, and the notion was pointless anyway; why would we want to be ferried back and forth a distance of a hundred yards? But it was a deeply satisfying fantasy: pull away the braided rug, lift the hidden trapdoor that would admit us to the roughly dug tunnel, board the little train with its six loaf-shaped cars, emerge into the fragrance of the night garden.

Are You Happy?

One afternoon Andy and I gathered armfuls of tulips with two-inch stems from the inn garden and brought them to our mother. Katy, babysitting for us that night under the supervision of a Williams student, told us that we could expect Chief Royal of the Williamstown police department to pull up in his sedan at any moment to question us about our theft of property. We wept and trembled. And once, walking along a gravel path in the garden, we heard a fluttering in the bushes. It was a rabbit giving birth, her eyes filmed over with shock and fear of us.

At some point—this must have been somewhat later—we appropriated a sack of sunflower seeds from the inn garden potting shed in order to feed a baby robin we'd rescued. (Because of some tangle of neural circuits, this recollection comes to me packed inside another memory, quite unrelated, of listening to a sermon by the Reverend William Sloane Coffin at the First Congregational Church.) I slung the burlap bag over my shoulder as we carried it across College Place, through the communal garden, and past the Barneses' house. The baby bird was far too young to feed on seeds, and it turned away from the egg yolk we offered in a medicine dropper. It began to puff up and drowse, and within a week it was dead. The seed bag must have sprung a leak as I carried it, because late in August a wavering line of sunflowers sprang up to trace our progress.

—

Accompanied by James, and wearing a black Spanish mantilla from the dress-up box, I liked to drop by the Williams Inn lobby and lounge. Because the inn was one of the few places my mother had put off-limits, Andy chose not to go along. I made my way through the lobby to the bar, where Williams alumni in lime green pants and madras jackets interrupted their sessions of joke-swapping to smile down on me indulgently. I proceeded to do my best to entertain them. Sometimes, not knowing quite how I'd brought it off, I scored a direct hit; the alums guffawed uproariously. I memorized these laugh lines and repeated them on subsequent visits.

For the amusement of my audience I put James through the series of tricks my father had taught him. "What do politicians do to babies?" I asked him. James licked my face obligingly and the circle of red-faced alums burst into approving applause. "Would you rather be dead or Republican?" I prompted. James lay down, rolled onto his back, and presented his belly. The reaction I got to this trick was equivocal and mystifying. Eyebrows shot up; there was an audible undercurrent like the grumbling in the House of Commons. Some laughed abruptly, a few stepped away, nobody clapped.

A few years later, when I'd grown too self-conscious to entertain the alums, I contented myself with spending my allowance at the Williams Inn gift shop. I knew their stock very well; mostly it was maple syrup and sugar, "Beautiful Berkshires" postcards in black and white, and blown-glass animal figurines. Nevertheless, I always made a show of browsing through the merchandise, keeping my back to the proprietress, who tended to glare. I remember the view out the small-paned window in that shop: the doorman and the boxy cars and in the distance, the blowing elms.

What I liked enough to buy were the mint chocolate miniatures, two for a penny, kept in a wicker basket on the counter, and the surprise balls. These were long streamers of multicolored crepe paper rolled up into a sphere about the size of a softball with small favors enclosed between the layers. I believe they cost a dime. I took my surprise ball across the street to my house, where I tore off the cellophane wrapper and rolled it like a bocce ball across my bedroom floor. It spilled little tin men and tiny American flags and crudely molded plastic starfish as it unspooled—useless prizes that expended their value the moment they were revealed.

———

I remember very little of my sister in the gray house. She was too sophisticated, I believed, to be expected to pay at-

tention to Andy and me, too busy listening to Pat Boone
singing "Love Letters in the Sand" on the radio in her room
and making entries in her padded, keyed diary to view us
with anything but irritation. I do remember that she explained to me that a movie was like a billboard with a picture
that moved and turned into other pictures; I hadn't yet seen
one, and it would be several years before my mother allowed
Andy and me to walk down to Spring Street on Saturday
evenings and pay a quarter to watch *Blue Denim* or *The Tin-
gler* in the midst of a mob of catcalling undergraduates at the
Walden Theatre. And I remember that more than once, she
and the Williams student who was our babysitter ordered us
peremptorily to bed, only to tease us by crawling under our
mattresses to buck us awake.

The babysitter's name was Brad Ordway. He was a tall,
goofy, talented boy who could cut frogs and wizards out of
tinfoil and play boogie-woogie on our mother's upright piano. Andy and I capered around the room and spun ourselves dizzy as he pounded out "St. James Infirmary." When
bedtime came I flattened myself on the living room floor,
eyes clamped shut, anticipating the moment when Brad Ordway would scoop me into his arms and carry me to my
room. Pressed closely against his chest, gently jolted by his
progress up the stairs, I fell into an erotic swoon.

Once, at Christmastime, when Brad Ordway made a joke
of catching me and kissing me under the mistletoe—he'd al-

ready given Katy her own decorous peck on the cheek—I got caught up in such a hysterical giggling panic that I knocked myself out by banging my head against the doorjamb. Or so Katy told me. I don't remember this incident at all.

Sex began by being all around me, in the sky and the trees, expanding like a gas. As I discovered its secrets, it slowly shrank and hardened, became solid and local rather than diffuse and general. I suppose this process roughly traces the Freudian ideal of progress toward genitality, but what I lost when I learned about sex had more to do with the world and how I received it than the body and how I felt it. The discovery of the body made sex come down out of the sky and the trees. It was as if the source of the agent that awoke and colored and brought the world to life and motion had been traced to a mechanical buzzing device in a corner of an abandoned shed.

—

I was a vulnerable child, more sinned against than sinning, but I knew what it was to feel the tug of sadistic arousal. An example: A fretful little boy named Bobby Prescott moved into the gray house after we had moved next door, to the white one. Andy and I scorned him. Once, horsing around in the yard, I grew irritated at the way he dug his fingernails into my forearm and deliberately kneed him in the groin. He ran shrieking to his mother, who dragged me into the kitchen and sat me down on a wooden chair, gripping my shoulders to restrain me from bolting. She advised me that in case I didn't know, a boy's testicles—she used that word, and I remember the deliberate way her mouth worked when she pronounced it—were his *Achilles' heel.* Mrs. Prescott was nervous and pretty, with a fringe of auburn bangs and a dancer's carriage. Like many of the faculty-wife mothers of my playmates, she never missed an opportunity to pass on a piece of enlightening information. Once, when I mentioned that my great-grandfather had been a Scotsman, she told me that during the war the members of the kilt-wearing Scottish brigades had been known as "the ladies from hell." I found this phrase so thrilling that I muttered it under my breath for weeks.

Dickie Barnes wasn't yet ten when he burned down a pine tree in his parents' yard. I remember that occasion because his mother arrived on our back doorstep in the middle of the afternoon and asked my mother to give her a drink. Dickie's punishment—which backfired, because he enjoyed it—was to sit in a bathtub filled with cold water and light an entire box of wooden kitchen matches. He made a practice of slashing open the crotches of stuffed animals with his Swiss army knife and inserting one-inch firecrackers into the resulting cavities. The scorched remnants of my rabbits and teddy bears littered the path through the lilacs that separated our house from the Barneses'.

Dickie was the author of several of my misfortunes. Once, in the woods, he dared me to swing on a tree vine over a deep culvert. The vine slid through my hands; I fell ten feet or so and landed heavily on my back, knocking both consciousness and wind out of myself. When I came to, gasping like a landed fish, Dickie was gone. He had run back to my house to tell my mother. "Emily's hurt" was his report. And one summer afternoon he accused me of jinxing a game of marbles by loitering in the doorway of the empty garage where it was being played. He warned me that if I didn't remove myself from his line of sight he would stab me in my bare foot with a ski pole, one of those old-fashioned ones with a floppy umbrella-shaped disk just above the point. I refused. Dickie made good on his threat and I limped home howling, the pole lodged between two small bones in my foot.

Looking at the list I've compiled of Dickie's offenses, I see I've made him sound like a sociopath, which he wasn't. If he had been born ten years ago instead of fifty-eight, he would surely have been put on medication before the end of first grade, but in those laissez-faire days he was considered merely a naughty boy. At any rate, it wasn't Dickie who was my nemesis but his brother Russell, just my age, quiet, self-contained, and effortlessly athletic, an excellent student with an ability to focus intently on math problems and puzzles and strategic board games. Even though we lived next to one another and shared the same classroom at school, Russell never quite acknowledged my existence. When he noticed me at all, it was with an air of mildly surprised contempt. Comparing myself to Russell, I began to understand that people's minds are very different. His was well-ordered and efficient. Mine, somehow, was not. This contrast would become still clearer to me in the years that followed, when I failed one math course after another in school.

Russell had a severe dignity, but he was not above entering into the games of doctor that Dickie instigated, using me as the patient. Dickie was the surgeon; it was he who lowered my underpants and poked at my genitals with a stick. Russell took the role of consultant, standing back a little and watching the procedure over Dickie's shoulder.

—

Gordon and Jessie Barnes were ten or twelve years older than my parents, representatives of a time before the G.I. Bill changed the composition of the Williams faculty and student body. Many years after we left Williamstown, my mother told me that she and my father had been surprised and grateful at the welcome the Barneses gave them when they moved to College Place. My parents were young, poor, and ambitious. My father's Jewishness was a novelty at Williams in those years. My mother was a bit of a bluestocking. The Barneses, with their antiques and oil paintings and peony bushes, seemed settled and established by the time they reached their forties.

Gordon Barnes was chairman of the Williams College art department, a hale, cheerful man with tufted eyebrows and a slight paunch. He was one of the first to use Metrecal, an early meal-replacement drink, which he decanted into an ornate ceramic beer mug. When a small child spoke to him he listened attentively, tilting his body and widening his round eyes.

Jessie Barnes was a willowy southerner with gray curls and an aristocratic air. She was kind and humorous but languid, with a habit of lying in bed late in the morning. She looked so tranquil and dignfied there, drinking coffee and paging through the *Berkshire Eagle,* her reading glasses perched low on her fine straight nose, that nobody could disapprove. And the bed itself was fresh and lavishly appointed, with a pearly satin coverlet and hand-embroidered pillowcases. Who could blame her for taking her leisure? She was, after all, the mother of Dickie, and three other boys as well.

I felt comfortable at the Barneses' house, which was both more formal and more relaxed than my own. Often, I let myself in without knocking. Early in the mornings Gordon stepped around me as I sat at the foot of the kitchen stairs, waiting for the boys to come down. He always greeted me the same way: "Hello, Seven-five-four Emily!" (This was our family's first phone number.) I chattered at him as he poured coffee and buttered toast for Jessie's tray. The Barneses' spaniel, Brownie, lay sprawled at my feet, her chin resting on her paws, her small shrewd eyes swivelling.

I last saw Jessie twenty-five years ago, when my mother and husband and I were invited to dinner at the Barneses' newly built retirement house in South Williamstown. (I couldn't help but disapprove of the way my parents' faculty friends tended to move from the heart of the campus to rusticate on the outskirts of the town as they aged. It was as if they had forgotten the specifics of their connection to the past, taking consolation for the loss by glutting themselves on the fungible loveliness of the valley and hills. They designed and built houses in high, remote meadows with walls of glass, the better to view the mountains. They put in gardens and installed lap pools; their limbs grew brown and sinewy as their hair turned white. The aging of these emeriti seemed ideal: healthy, serene, contemplative. But as far as I was concerned, it wasn't Williamstown they had retired to; it was the Beautiful Berkshires.) At the end of the evening Jessie took me aside in the kitchen and advised me to get my mother's car keys out of her purse while she was distracted. She wouldn't like that, I said. She always insists on driving. Not if you make it a fait accompli, Jessie whispered. She gripped my wrist with her arthritic hand and looked me hard in the eye, challenging me to take charge, to act like an adult.

I last saw Gordon at my mother's interment next to my father's grave in a South Williamstown cemetery with a view of the mountains. Jessie, too, had died, a day before my mother, and Gordon had come here immediately after her burial. He was wearing a long dark coat and a muffler on this raw February day. His tufted eyebrows had turned white and sprouted into wild thickets; otherwise he looked much the same. Cheerfulness had always run so deep in his personality that he seemed unable to shake it, even in these circumstances. He made some remark about funeral-hopping that would have been jarring had it come from someone whose acceptance of grief was less unresisting and complete.

—

In a snapshot taken when I was seven, I stand between Katy, then thirteen, and Andy, six. Katy, who in earlier photographs had a burdened, anxious air, gazes confidently—even a little flirtatiously—into the camera. Andy, who had been a drooling, beaming cherub only a few years earlier, has become a boy. I'm heavy and sheepish in my stiff-skirted party dress and patent leather Mary Janes. My eyes are lowered; my bare legs are spotted with scratched-open mosquito bites; my hair has lost its early curls, and my smile is gummy and wounded. Though I don't remember feeling unhappy at the time this photograph was taken, I can see—looking at it now—that I had become newly and painfully unattractive, and knew it. I was in school now, and not doing well.

This was the era of "The Ballad of the Harp-Weaver." I dogged my mother around the house, begging her to read this grisly old Edna St. Vincent Millay standard aloud to me, even though—as she often pointed out—I was quite capable of reading it to myself. I was fascinated by the tableau of the over-grown, emaciated son reclining in his starving mother's lap—

A-rock-rock-rocking,
    To a mother-goose rhyme!
Oh, but we were happy
For half an hour's time!

—and the spectral mother, weaving clothes for her son on a loom that was also a harp "with a woman's head." This never failed to make me weep:

She wove a red cloak
    So regal to see,
"She's made it for a king's son,"
I said, "and not for me."
But I knew it was for me.

I cried a good deal when I was young, but my tears were not the straightforwardly inconsolable tears of childhood. Instead, they were the manifestation of a particularly satisfying kind of lyrical sadness. I sang through tears as my mother and I sat at the piano. I wept when we took walks together on summer evenings to admire a new moon. I found I could induce these tears by imagining my mother and me as we might be seen from a great distance, by thinking of my childhood as if I were looking back at it from the vantage point of a time when she was gone and the songs we sang forgotten.

All through my childhood I cultivated these pleasant states of melancholy; they drew me closer to my mother. I felt that my tears pleased her, and when I was done crying I wiped my eyes and ran outside to play.

—

A few years ago I returned to College Place. I already knew, of course, that the college had long since gone coeducational. I knew that Williams students were no longer the beer-swilling fraternity louts so many of them had been in the fifties, when their professors could be counted on to award them the gentleman's C, and faculty wives warned their children to stay away from them after dark, and James Finney Baxter, the president of the college, in a moment of exasperation after a homecoming-weekend incident, denounced them all as "fornicating earthworms." But somehow I wasn't quite prepared to acknowledge that the dangerous young gods of my childhood had turned seventy now, and that the current crop of students milling around the freshman quad were the age of their grandchildren. They were a carefully assembled assortment of young people of both genders and many colors; some wore their hair in dreadlocks, some in buzz cuts, others in lank ponytails. The ones I saw that day had the docile, put-upon look of students everywhere, slogging through spring slush to their classes, weighed down like sherpas with overloaded backpacks.

I knew that College Place had been blocked off opposite the library, and I knew that the two houses I grew up in had become college buildings. But on this latest visit, when I walked around to the back of the gray house, I saw that the lilac bushes and the little yard where Dickie Barnes suggested to me that I pat the bumblebee were gone. A diagonal walkway connected the Barneses' house to the gray house, and both buildings had together become something called the Center for Environmental Studies. I was puzzled and distressed by this transformation; it was like visiting a pair of beloved maiden aunts and finding that they had been recruited by a cult.

The white house was now "contract housing" for the college. The side yard had become a parking lot; fire escapes and a handicapped ramp had been installed. Now that it had

been annexed by the college, the house looked discolored
and diminished, like a dead tooth. The chestnut trees were
gone, replaced by full-grown pines. And where was the circular driveway?

I climbed the steps to the front porch, found a buzzer
system, and pressed a button at random. Just as I was about
to give up and return to my car, a groggy student in sweat-
pants and flip-flops appeared at the door, nodding absently at
my attempts to apologize for awakening him. It's just that I
used to live here when I was a child many years ago, I explained, and I was curious to see . . . But the student had
turned his back on me and walked away, leaving me alone in
the silent hall and free to wander through the house.

The house would no longer permit much wandering. On
either side of the hall, where high open archways once led
into twin living rooms, were plywood doors plastered with
concert posters and bumper stickers. Student rooms. The
hall floor was covered with indoor-outdoor carpet and the
walls had been painted an institutional gray-green. I climbed
the staircase, which retained its original banister under a
coat of blistering varnish. A kind of glassed-in kiosk faced
me from the second-floor landing, covered with pastel flyers
and sign-up sheets for chores. The bedrooms on the second
floor were all locked, inhabited by students now, but I recognized the central hall. When I climbed up to the third
floor, where the attic used to be, and my mother's sewing

room, and the big tent-ceilinged room I was allowed to move into when I was eleven—the one with a window that looked down on the gray house and the library and the elms—I found myself in an unfamiliar narrow, twisting hallway, with many doors on either side, utterly disoriented.

I turned and walked back down the stairs to the ground floor, to the part of the house that was still used communally. The kitchen was recognizably the one where my mother used to serve macaroni and cheese to Andy and me at a round yellow Formica table when we walked home from school at lunchtime on winter days. While we ate, she stood at that counter by the sink (still there!) and smoked a Pall Mall as she wrote out her grocery list, one foot drawn up storkstyle and parked above her knee. The surfaces were cluttered with cereal boxes now, and rows of empty beer bottles waiting to be recycled. The kitchen looked institutionally shabby but anatomically unchanged, except that the butler's pantry where my mother kept her wineglasses and copper molds and soup tureens was now an indentation in the wall, occupied by a washer and dryer.

My mother spent whole days in that kitchen preparing for the ambitious dinner parties she managed on my father's meager salary and served in the adjacent dining room, which was still itself, too, I was happy to see, still an airy, high-ceilinged rectangle with four tall windows. The walls were an insipid pale blue now: how many different colors had they been painted in the last fifty years? When we lived here the dining room was purple, an unusual dusky shade, very original and daring for those days. That room was my mother's special project. She hung the windows with bamboo roll-up blinds that cooled and dappled the light so that at dusk the sherry in the decanter on the sideboard took on an interior shimmer. She was aiming at a certain high-bohemian elegance, and she achieved it. It was in this room, on a narrow teak table, that she served her pâtés and fish dishes cooked in parchment and garlicky green salads (in the French way, after the main course) and her rum-infused *pots-de-crème*.

This room was the scene of my parents' early triumphs. My brother and sister and I were banished to the second floor when my parents entertained. We stole down to the stair landing and watched. Sometimes, during the cocktail hour, my mother beckoned to us and we were allowed to join the party in our pajamas for a half hour, and to pass a tray of puff-pastry hors d'oeuvres. Then the guests filed in pairs through the glass French doors (still there) into the dining room, where we could barely see the goings on, though we could hear swellings of laughter and my father's voice rising over all the others as he told stories and pronounced judgments.

I walked through the kitchen to the mudroom in back, where my father used to soak Kirby cucumbers in brine-filled ceramic crocks to approximate the pickles of his Philadelphia childhood. It had always been unheated, but now it was semiderelict, a storage room for bikes and cross-country ski equipment. The back door was nailed shut with two crossed boards, and peering through the glass I could see that the back porch was completely tumbledown now, no longer used. That porch was where the milkman left our twice-a-week gallon, with its three inches of cream on top, and where icicles as long and thick as my leg hung in rows from the steeply pitched roof. Peering out at the peeling paint on the steps, I was hit by a sense of the past that made the breath catch in my throat. I remembered the sensation of slamming through the screen door and bursting out into the morning, which smelled of the cold and the old snow and fresh car exhaust from the Williams Inn parking lot—the smell of all my life in store.

Are You Happy?

I learned to read at three, or so the story goes. This happened very suddenly in a second-floor room in the Williamstown public library. While my mother browsed through the adult fiction shelves on the ground floor, I sat in a rocking chair in front of a big fan-shaped window looking at the very familiar pages of *The Little Engine That Could*. That day in the library, words began to move under my eyes. Like the little engine chugging her way up the hill, I found I could push printed marks into meaning through the force of my mind. I thought I could, I thought I could, and then, indeed, I could.

Or at least I thought I could. Now I suspect that I was less an early reader than I was a prodigious memorizer, or at least that the line between memorization and active reading was less clear than the public-library epiphany has made it seem. But whether or not I really read at three, my mother believed I could, and I did legitimately learn to read before I went to school. My early reading represented a victory for my mother's permissive child-rearing philosophy. Until I began to fail in school, this distinction gave me some protection from my father's perpetual annoyance. I was chaotic and exasperating, but I was my mother's gifted child. For a while I enjoyed a gifted child's prerogatives.

I remember the books I "read" during this period mostly for their illustrations. I can see Ferdinand drowsing under the cork tree, its branches hung with bunches of corks (I was too young to get the joke), and Peter hiding from Farmer MacGregor in the watering can. I can see the young rabbit in *Wait Till the Moon Is Full* lying in his mother's arms in their underground burrow, and the festive party that the rabbit community held above ground in the soft, grainy light of the full moon, rendered with tiny dots. There was a rabbit carrying a parasol, a rabbit wearing a straw boater in the style of Matisse, a rabbit on a unicycle. I remember the schematically flat but deeply shadowed black-and-yellow Paris of *Madeline:* the old house covered in vines, the twelve little girls in two straight lines, the alarming red ambulance parked askew in the center of the page, the doll's house from Papa and Miss Clavell running "fast and faster," her streaming habit resolving into a stylishly emphatic abstract line, like the tail of my father's signature.

What text I can recall I hear being read in my mother's distinctive low voice, with its edge of cigarette rasp. Andy is absent from these memories, though I know for a fact that my mother read to both of us. What I seem to have chosen to remember is simply my mother and me: the comfort of sprawling in her lap, my head resting against her breathing bosom, feeling the hum of her voice in the bones of my face.

All through my childhood, my reading was bound up with my mother. Under her direction I read all the childhood classics and many adult books as well. Among our favorites were the Pooh books, *Little Women* and *Otto of the Silver Hand,* and, later, *Le Morte D'Arthur.* By the time I was eight I was consuming two or three books a week. When I was ten I was reading more, having more or less given up by then on the competing claims of homework. I would finish a book one day; when I came home from school the next I'd find another—sometimes resting on my pillow.

I was a fast, omnivorous reader. I loved to read, but in truth I've never really been a full member of the tribe of bookish people. I'm tempted to say that I loved life more than books, but it would be more accurate to say that it was words that I loved more. My own words, that is—the ones into which I was continuously converting my experiences.

There were certain books of which my mother disapproved. She had mysterious doubts about *Mary Poppins.* She was less than enthusiastic about *The Wind in the Willows* and discouraged me from reading *Black Beauty.* She preferred *Jane Eyre* to *Wuthering Heights* (so do I). She put the Nancy Drew mysteries emphatically off-limits. I never opened the covers of one of these until I was twenty and found a collection one summer in a cabin in the Adirondacks. Lying on a lumpy cot through a week of rainy afternoons, I read them eagerly, looking to discover what it was about Nancy and her roadster and her chums that my mother found so censorable. I could only conclude that it was the cozy banality of these books that she disliked.

My mother and I never discussed my reading: that was not her way, and I was much too young then to know it was mine. The books she gave me were different from the books I read for school. They served no didactic purpose; they were offered to me simply for my pleasure, and—I sensed—for another reason I couldn't quite fathom but was glad to accept on faith. My mother was always cool and offhand; she had a horror of intrusiveness. But I knew the books she left me were markers along a meandering trail that she meant me to follow. I hoped that when I reached the end I might find her there.

—

I was sent for half days to Mrs. Imhoff's nursery school, where I learned to pump high on the swings and was unfairly spanked for having wet my pants when in fact I had sat in a puddle. I think it was there that I met Eileen Mannion, who was the first child I ever played with who lived away from College Place. We sat on the floor in Eileen's bedroom, each with a square of sketching paper and a box of crayons. Eileen told me to watch her carefully and to draw exactly what she drew. This was intolerable, but I did as she said. Then, as a defiant afterthought, I outlined my inexpertly copied horse heavily with a black crayon. You weren't supposed to do that, said Eileen, and yanked the drawing away from me. I began to cry. This was the way most of our encounters ended, but we maintained our association until we were six or seven, when one day Eileen called my name and I failed to answer. "You must be deaf," she told me. "I can't be friends with a deaf person." That was the end, though we did revive our friendship several years later.

I have only three memories of my kindergarten year, all distinct and nearly without context. The first is a happy one of rooting noisily through a box of primitive percussion instruments: triangles, gourds on sticks, crudely stitched Indian-style drums decorated with stiff turkey feathers dyed yellow and green. I remember choosing a pair of oversized cymbals with bulbous wooden handles and marching around the room with my classmates to the exhilarating rhythm of "The Monkey Wrapped His Tail Around the Flagpole." The second is a memory of rolling off the stage into the orchestra pit during a performance of *Sleeping Beauty*—I played the title role, and actually fell asleep as I lay on the floor awaiting Prince Charming. The third is of a brawl with a birthday boy during a classroom party. My mother had bought a pair of cap guns and a beautiful holster hung with white vinyl fringes and inlaid with walnut-sized glass rubies and emeralds—I can see it now—for me to give as a present. I understood what presents were, having received them myself, but when it came time to hand the guns and holster over, I found that I couldn't. Punches were thrown; the boy and I fell to the floor and were separated by the teacher.

—

During the summer between kindergarten and first grade, Gordon Barnes's younger sister Dorothy came to visit. She wore tailored, cinch-waisted suits and strode through rooms confidently, like a career woman from a forties movie. My mother admired her dashing clothes and the high polish of her grooming. Dorothy was working on a degree in psychology. She recruited me as a subject because she needed to administer IQ tests to a certain number of children in order to fulfill some requirement, or so my mother told me later. Just as I harbor suspicions about my early reading, so I suspect that this was a cover story. I believe the test was my mother's idea, that she arranged it because on the one hand she was anxious to confirm her sense that my mind was superior and on the other to be relieved of her obscure fear that my mind was defective.

Dorothy sat me down in the Barneses' dining room. She had arranged the materials of the test in squared-off piles, doubled in depth by the reflective polished surface of the table. Her fingernails were riveting, just short of talon-length and painted a deep purplish red. Her smile was moist and cautiously encouraging. I remember Dorothy but very little else about that afternoon, and I can't be sure that what I do recall dates from this incident or from later occasions when I was put through batteries of psychological tests. I do have a clear memory of being asked to interpret pictures of interpersonal scenes. There was a little girl in pigtails standing in a doorway with her back to the viewer, looking up at a tall man whose face was invisible: only his long trousered legs were shown. There was a woman holding a mirror in one hand and an apple in the other.

What happened, apparently—I don't remember this at

all and have only my mother's version—was that I did very well on the early, verbal portion of the test, balked a little at the puzzles Dorothy asked me to construct, burst into tears and ran out of the Barneses' house when she confronted me with a number problem. My mother took me out of first grade that fall and enrolled me in Pine Cobble, Williamstown's only private elementary school.

—

Every weekday morning in the middle and late nineteen fifties I stood in a line of children pausing on the wooden porch of Pine Cobble School as John Steele, the elderly custodian, detained us for a moment to brush the soles of our shoes clean. He received each of us in turn, crouching down to engage our eyes with a look of baffling intensity. "Are you happy?" he asked, and waited, head cocked, until each child answered in the affirmative. Then he did his business with the whisk broom and let us go.

John Steele was one of those lean, hardworking loners who seem to have disappeared from the world in recent times. He had been subjecting Pine Cobble students to his daily interrogation for many years before I became a student there and maintained the tradition until the year before my family left Williamstown, when he died. A small obituary appeared in the mimeographed school bulletin. John Steele was a familiar figure around the halls of the school, the piece began, and even at age eleven I understood that the author—probably the overeducated school secretary—was straining to say something, anything at all, about this disagreeable old man who hobbled through the narrow corridors muttering imprecations under his breath. He had no home as far as any of us could see, only the supply closet, reeking of wintergreen disinfectant, where he kept his mops and buckets. The eulogist concluded by invoking the phrase for which John Steele was known:

"'Are you happy?' A very important question, and one which, from time to time, we should all remember to ask our children."

Even if adults found it convenient to believe that John Steele's motives were kind, I knew they were not. I knew that he was quite deliberately putting an old-fashioned scare into us, getting his own back at our expense. When I grew old enough to imagine such things, I pictured his childhood as having been spent in a grim row house in a desolate upstate New York town, with a brute for a father and a thin, sour mother and a square of oilcloth on the kitchen table. When I reached the age of interpretation I understood that John Steele's question was an expression of contempt for us, a sarcastic commentary on the softness of the lot of Pine Cobble students—we with our thermoses full of cream of tomato soup and our parents full of high expectations for our lives.

When I first arrived at Pine Cobble I hated the inescapable audience with John Steele that started each school day. I dreaded the moment when it would be my turn to be ushered into his hands, feeling one of them fall heavily on my shoulder while the other fumbled down past my knee to find and grip my ankle. By the time I left Pine Cobble, I had hardened myself to the ordeal. In fact I learned to enjoy it. I liked to watch John Steele embarrass and frighten the other children. When his cataract-clouded stare made first-graders cry, I congratulated myself on my superior toughness. When pubescent sixth-grade girls bristled with defiance at the insolent familiarity of his touch, I thanked my lucky stars that I was still flat-chested and square-waisted. I learned to hang around in the doorway for as long as I could after he was done with me in hopes of seeing him take on some of the older boys, the ones who were my tormentors. Sometimes these boys tried to clown their way out of the encounter— "I'm *happy,* I'm *happy!*" they would cry out preemptively, and dance a little evasive jig as his eyes and hands fell on them—but John Steele was having none of it. For the five or ten seconds he detained each student on the porch, he imposed a rough equality I couldn't help but welcome. Unlike our teachers, he never played favorites. He made us understand that he cordially hated every one of us.

—

Take away God, Latin, the cane, class distinctions and sex-ual taboos," wrote George Orwell in his memoir of his days in a British public school, "and the fear, the hatred, the snob-bery and the misunderstanding might still all be there." Look-ing back at my own school experience I can report that, yes, the fear and hatred and snobbery and misunderstanding were indeed still there. Orwell's conditions can't fully be met, of course, because class distinctions and sexual taboos have never been eliminated anywhere in the world, and never will be. I have to acknowledge as well that at least for most of the time I was there, Pine Cobble was not an adequate test case for Orwell's hypothesis: even though no religious training was imposed on us and corporal punishment had lost official sanction, it was hardly a progressive school. In fact, Pine Cobble modeled itself in part on the kind of British public school Orwell wrote about. There was the same obsession with sports: students with athletic talent were celebrated and pudgy uncoordinated children like me were openly de-plored. And just as at Orwell's Crossgates, there was an ethic of Darwinian survivalism at Pine Cobble that encouraged the strong to torment the weak.

When I say "the weak," I mean myself. I was a natural mark for teasing with my fat stomach and scalloped gums and show-off's vocabulary and the no-brand barrel staves my father ordered from the Montgomery Ward catalog instead of the Head skis that popular children owned. No other child was teased as much and as constantly as I was, and the teasing got worse every year until sixth grade, when it lessened and then briefly disappeared. But I knew it wasn't just these obvious liabilities that made me the leading pariah at Pine Cobble: there were other fat children, other faculty brats who wore home-sewn clothes and carried egg salad sandwiches on whole wheat bread to school, and though they were certainly teased, they were left alone most of the time. Some were even respected. It was something less easily definable that made me the object of this constant, savage derision. Perhaps it had to do with the gap between my obviously high opinion of my own intelligence and my poor performance in nearly all of my classes.

During the years I was a student there, Pine Cobble grew steadily less and less like Orwell's Crossgates. Many of the faculty wives who had placed their children in the school also joined the faculty with an eye toward reforming and modernizing it from the inside. The wives lobbied against corporal punishment and the use of exercise as punishment. They tried (but failed) to abolish after-school study hall. They did their best to discourage discrimination on the basis of clothing: children who teased other children for wearing ankle socks rather than kneesocks, or corduroy jumpers rather than pleated wool skirts from the House of Walsh, were taken aside and gently reasoned with. More generally, the wives—for a while my mother was one of them—tried to introduce a revised set of values to the children. They taught that happiness should not be sought in a primitive glorying in strength and pleasure and luck and looks but in concern for others and the full development of one's own capacities.

But while the faculty wives managed to end most of the worst practices and traditions at Pine Cobble, they made little headway against fear, hatred, snobbery, and misunderstanding among the children. In fact, their efforts only made the cruelty problem worse—at least for me. As the official cruelty of the Orwellian cane was slowly withdrawn from the classroom, the unofficial cruelty of the corridors and schoolyard grew and filled its place. Better to live under a strong bad regime than a weak good one—better for me, at least. I learned this at Pine Cobble. Orwell wouldn't have shared this view, but he would have understood it. And so would John Steele, who I'm sure had nothing but contempt for the ideas and intentions of the faculty wives, if he ever thought about them at all. One morning, when I was sent by a teacher on an errand to an outbuilding, I caught a glimpse of him on the porch, bending over to knock his arthritic knee into alignment with a wooden mallet. His face was locked in a snarling wince. I saw that, for him, the only reliable happiness was a stoical acceptance of pain.

—

The year that my mother was homeroom teacher for my fifth-grade class was my worst at Pine Cobble. That fall the boys were all hit at once with a mammary obsession, and she made a fatal early error by assigning Breasted's *Ancient Times*. The snickering lasted through Thanksgiving, and once the name Breasted had lost its hilarious novelty, they moved on to playground speculations about my mother's bra size and made remarks in my presence about her breath and the color of her tobacco-stained teeth.

And just as all that began to fade, my mother made a cataclysmic misjudgment. Stephen Flagg, a big rowdy boy who sat in the back row with others of his kind, was disrupting the class one day with rude noises. My mother paused at the blackboard—she had been ignoring Stephen—and turned to face us. "Stephen," she said, "perhaps you'd like to come up here and entertain the class."

Stephen was all too happy to oblige: he sauntered to the front of the classroom, yanked his shirttail loose, inserted his cupped palm in his armpit, and went to work, producing a volley of highly amplified, wet-sounding armpit farts. The class exploded in whoops and cheers. Encouraged, Stephen stepped up the pace of his performance, pumping his arm triumphantly. The boys in the back joined in with their own efforts; a call-and-response rhythm established itself and the class settled in for an extended saturnalia. My mother stood with her back against the blackboard, her arms crossed against her chest. Her mouth was slightly open, her whitened lips drawn back tightly against her teeth, like a frantic cornered cat preparing to hiss. I knew why the boys felt free to treat her with such open disrespect: it was because she was my mother. I knew she knew this too. I kept my head down, glancing up once or twice, afraid to meet her eyes.

—

Pine Cobble was run by a married couple called the Frittses. I find it hard to place them on either side of the traditional/ progressive divide. Douglas Fritts I don't remember at all. In my mind he's simply a male body in a tweed jacket with a blank oval for a face—no voice, no mannerisms. Once he brought me an oversized cherry lollipop when I was home in bed with the flu. It was a skating prize, the only prize I ever received in all my years at school. I had won it unknowingly and by default, simply by staying inside the two lines of barrels laid out on the ice to establish the boundaries of the race.

Mrs. Fritts—odd that I remember her much better than her husband, but have forgotten her first name—was a trim woman in her forties with short, curly dark hair, who wore her reading glasses on a twinkling chain around her neck. Her walk was bouncy and she exuded a Buddha-like calm. Every day at recess she toured the schoolyard in her tennis shoes, humming airs from Mozart and smiling at every student she encountered with a steady, distant benevolence. The humming was an evasive tactic; it was as if she walked in time to some celestial tune unheard by anyone else. As long as the music played she stayed in motion, and nothing could stop her. "I'm simply doing my rounds," her manner announced, "and I'm determined to be pleased by everything I see." When she came upon a tearful child or a fight or an incident of bullying she waltzed her way around it, giving a conductor's nod to the teacher whose responsibility it was to take note of the problem.

The Frittses were a musical family. Their cello-playing daughter Peg was in my class, a slender, studious girl with long brown braids. I envied everything about her, even her no-nonsense name. She was never quite popular—her shyness and her parentage ruled that out—but the boys who tormented me respected her and let her pass unmolested. I can see Peg now, perched on a folding chair on the makeshift stage of the outbuilding where assemblies and recitals were held, dwarfed by her cello as she gripped it between her poignantly knobby knees, her head lowered devotedly. *Now, that's the way to be,* I thought as I watched her.

My sister played the piano and so did my mother, though

a little perfunctorily. I had been sent to a piano teacher myself, but soon I began to wander off into the woods on my way to my lessons on Southworth Street and the idea was dropped. When I envied Peg, I knew I had nobody to blame but myself. Sometimes I find myself trying out the idea that my mother was at fault for failing to keep after me. But in the end I reject it: my mother saw very early that I was good at words and not much else. How can I blame her for knowing me so well?

But even so—my self-pity wells up reliably when I get onto this subject—being good at words was not much help when I was a misfit at Pine Cobble. Nobody could see the purely internal process of turning experience into words; if anything it tends to make a person look dim-witted. I had nothing to show for it. Unlike my schoolmate Tom Sommers, whose confiscated drawings of Messerschmitts and Fokkers were passed around and admired in the teacher's lounge, my verbal sketches stayed inside my head. Even in English, by far my best subject, my classroom performance was erratic; I was much stronger in vocabulary than in spelling and mechanics, and I had a tendency to combine words or coin new ones. One of these was "eithren," a substitute for "either" or "even," which I invented when I was four or five and stubbornly insisted on using until I was eight.

And to the degree that my aptitude for words showed itself in the classroom, I made myself an object of suspicion.

A student who did well in vocabulary and written expression but took years to learn her times tables and seemed unable to retain the fact that Trenton is the capital of New Jersey was considered not gifted but lazy and glib. Words were not mine in the way that Peg's cello was hers and Tom's charcoals and sketchpads were his. I had no special claim on them, and hoarding them in my vocabulary seemed like an illegitimate appropriation of the currency that everyone used.

I watched as Peg advanced steadily in her mastery of her instrument and the musical literature, her parents and teachers smiling and nodding and tapping their feet all the while. There was no comparable way to measure and reward the progress I was making with words, though I suppose I might have gotten some praise from adults if I had thought to write stories or poems. But for some reason that never occurred to me until much later. My writing remained purely internal.

It was this activity, and not woolgathering, that accounted for the absent look on my face that drove my teachers crazy. I felt an odd guilt about my internal writing that I don't believe I would have felt if I had been fantasizing rather than diarizing. "Emily," said my teachers, "get your head out of the clouds. Pay attention." But my head was rarely in the clouds during school hours, and I was nearly always paying attention—paying attention, for example, to my fifth-grade civics teacher's resemblance to a weasel or a stoat.

I played this internal writing game to comfort and amuse myself. I've continued to do it all my life, though it comes and goes. It went away, for example, when I reached the second semester of my fifth-grade year, or at least it mutated into something quite different and far less playful. My pronouns changed: "I" became "she" and my internal diary-keeping degenerated into a mechanical chronicle of my actions as I performed them. This was a jamming device, a noise I made to drown out the sounds of teasing that came from the outside and the conscious acknowledgment of that teasing that came from the inside: *Now she is walking into the cloakroom and putting on her jacket. Now she is pulling on her mittens. Now she is walking out the door to the porch, going down the steps, walking past the jungle gym.*

———

Pine Cobble was housed in a rambling gingerbread house at the southern end of the Williams campus. I have trouble sorting out my memories of the years I spent there sequentially but I can follow my mind's eye along the scuffed wainscoting of the narrow, curving halls and down the shaft of the central staircase, where lines of bobbing brown and blond heads moved up and down in steady streams between classes. I remember the room where we kept our lunch boxes and coats and galoshes in fifth grade, the year that my mother was our teacher, and the clamor in that room when we were let out for recess: the flying elbows, the shouts and taunts, the orange-peel-and-sour-milk smells, and the odor of vegetable soup that closely packed groups of children give off.

We were forbidden to climb the stairway to the third floor because the music teacher lived in a mysterious apartment up there with his peevish, reclusive wife and a yapping Lhasa apso. Art Siegenthal was the founding member of a local Dixieland band, an unpleasant man in his forties with a high jutting belly and a pompadour of shining dark hair that rose from the crown of his balding head. I sensed that he was considered slightly disreputable by the Frittses, that in their eyes he was redeemed only by his membership in the fraternity of music. (And indeed, years later I caught a glimpse of his band huddling together in a cold parking lot during a concert intermission, passing a joint.) Every morning he descended those forbidden stairs, nattily turned out in a navy blue blazer with gold buttons, a tuning fork in his breast pocket, and walked straight down the middle of the narrow corridor to the teachers' lounge. Our job was to stay out of his way.

I remember the sixth-grade classroom of Miss Bond. She was an English spinster in her sixties who wore what must have been one of the last whalebone corsets in the world under her starched high-collared blouse. Miss Bond had been teaching for forty years, in this country and in England, so she could tell us with authority that our British counterparts were very much our superiors. For one thing, they were capable of appreciating Miss Bond's dedication. She read us testimonials from bankers and university professors, expressing gratitude for her high expectations and firm guiding hand. Everything British was better: tea, literature, pedagogy, woolens, breeds of dog, newspapers. Our *Berkshire Eagle* was a poor thing compared to the *Manchester Guardian,* which she brought into class so that we could run our fingers over its onionskin paper, which turned translucent—she demonstrated—when held up to the window. It was only many years later, when I was fully adult and beyond Miss Bond's influence, that it occurred to me to wonder what it was about the paper that the overseas edition of the *Manchester Guardian* was printed on that made it so superior.

Posture was her obsession: it was the key, she told us, to self-respect. She lined us up against the walls on three sides of the room under the blackboards and passed us in review, identifying our weak points, our bowed legs and hunched shoulders. Once—probably more than once, but my memory has been kind enough to consolidate these incidents into one recollection—she poked me in the abdomen with her forefinger and stage-whispered, "Perhaps you wouldn't be quite so *lazy* if you weren't quite so *fat.*"

What she taught us I mostly forget. What I do remember is the poetry that she read aloud with a theatrical intensity

that embarrassed and fascinated me. She read John Mase-
field's "Sea Fever," which left me cold, and Alfred Noyes's
"The Highwayman," which thrilled me, especially the dark
red love-knot in the long dark hair of the innkeeper's black-
eyed daughter and the *tlot-tlot* of the hooves of the approaching highwayman's horse. Her rendition of Vachel Lindsay's
"The Congo" was mortifyingly uninhibited. She stalked the
classroom, eyes bulging, palms thrown up in the air, and fingers spread wide like a mime's. The boys in the back row,
who snickered at most of her performances, howled at this
one. Miss Bond had gone into trance.

. . . Mumbo-Jumbo, God of the Congo . . .
Mumbo-Jumbo will hoo-doo you.

At some point during the year we were taken to Chapin
Hall on the Williams campus to hear a visiting jazz band. This
was a schoolwide expedition—probably Art Siegenthal's idea.
Sitting ramrod straight at the end of her row of fourth-grade
charges, Miss Bond seemed unamused by the spectacle.
"Barrel-house kings, with feet unstable," who

Sagged and reeled and pounded on the table,
Pounded on the table,
Beat an empty barrel with the handle of a broom . . .

were one thing, apparently. Portly black men from Laurel, Mississippi, who bobbed and swayed and slapped a bass fiddle were another. Still, when we returned to the classroom, Miss Bond acknowledged that whatever one thought of that music, those men certainly seemed to be working very hard.

When we came back from Christmas vacation Miss Bond had discovered Paul Gallico's *The Snow Goose*. She brought a pile of copies of this slender novella into class and passed them out reverently. She held her own open to the title page and moved around the room, asking each child to notice and admire the print and the creamy paper. It was, she told us, a very beautiful book and a very touching story.

Oyster marshes, a wild sea, a tormented hunchback, a wounded bird, a frightened, inarticulate young girl: now, here was a formula. A year or even a few months earlier I would have fallen hard for it, but because I had come to hate Miss Bond, I struggled to resist the allure of *The Snow Goose*. It would be many years before I acquired a critical vocabulary, but if I had had one then I would have called it a piece of high-Romantic schlock. The feelings it evoked were big, smooth, and uniform, like the uppercase letters in the Palmer alphabet. I also suspected that under her whalebone corset Miss Bond was a vulgar sentimentalist, the kind whose tender feelings extend only to stock characters and predictable situations. Rumor had that she had ended up in this unsatisfactory country because of a failed romance, and when I read *The Snow Goose,* I hypothesized that in Miss Bond's mind, the brooding lighthouse keeper was a figure for the man who broke her heart.

And of course I understood that the reason Miss Bond never favored me, even though I was an advanced reader and had (of course) a large vocabulary, was not that I was disorganized and sloppy and late to pass in homework but that I was not enough like Fritha: not waifish and ethereal but pudgy and solid, with a homemade bowl haircut. I was unidealizable.

———

No one," Orwell writes, "can look back on his school days and say with truth that they were altogether unhappy." He writes about his moments of happiness at Crossgates, at liberty for an hour on summer mornings to read in the "sunlit sleeping dormitory," free to wander the grounds on summer afternoons and dredge the ponds for "enormous newts with orange-colored bellies."

And it's true: I can't say that I was unhappy during my days at Pine Cobble. The school building itself was the scene of constant and repeated failures, but I was as joyful as any other child when it was time to be let out for recess. Even though I knew I would have to walk through a barrage of taunts on my way to the swings, I also knew that once I had pumped high enough to be able to look down on the heads of the other children, I would be happy.

On every school day my real happiness began at the moment when I was released into the reviving waters of my Williamstown life like a gasping, flopping trout tossed over the side of a boat. I walked down Main Street under the elms past the yellow brick fraternity buildings where pledges were cruelly hazed. (All through my childhood I heard stories about these practices, most of them surely apochryphal: Did the brothers really urinate on the pledges? Force them to eat insects? Pull down their pants and make them sit in snowbanks? I liked to believe these legends were true, because that made me feel less alone in my torments at school. And I liked the idea of initiation, because it promised a moment of acceptance at the end of a series of trials.)

On spring and fall days, and on winter afternoons when I hadn't been kept in study hall until dusk, I spent an hour or two roaming around before I went home. During the school day I managed to contain my internal dialogues, but freedom loosened things inside me and I talked and sang to myself as I wandered. These utterances would have made no continuous sense to any listener; they were broken expostulations directed at myself or imagined companions, burst of enthusiasm, snatches of song refrains. Once when I was loitering in front of one of the Williams Inn annexes, admiring a Rolls-Royce parked there, running my hands along its fenders and muttering adjectives like "elegant" and "glossy," I was deeply embarrassed to realize that the elderly couple who owned it had been standing on the annex porch all the while, listening to me. "You like the car?" asked the man, smiling and jingling his keys. I turned and ran.

Sometimes I took a private tour of the greenroom at the Williamstown Theatre, where the makeup man once drew eyebrows on my mother's singed forehead with a grease pencil because the oven had exploded in her face an hour before she was due to address the League of Women Voters. Sometimes I walked around the freshman quadrangle, where the students played lacrosse. On Friday afternoons the students gathered to meet the bus that brought their dates from Vassar and Mount Holyoke. I watched as the girls in their pastel sweater sets and circle pins were handed down the steps by a uniformed driver. Williams boys surrounded the bus in a jostling semicircle; as each one's date appeared, the others would shove him forward to receive her.

Sometimes I visited the basement of Lehman Hall. It was a big, dank, low-ceilinged, fascinating place, littered with piles of rust-streaked mattresses and wooden desks scarred with initials and bad words that I added to my vocabulary without knowing exactly what they meant. It smelled of beer, mildew, and urine; the only light was a little watery sun straining through dusty window slits at ground level. One afternoon I heard feet thundering down the basement stairs from the dormitory first floor; that gave me enough warning to overturn an armchair and squat under it. Cursing and laughing, three barefoot students in shorts came spilling into the basement and rooted around in the shadows with a flashlight, searching for something. For a moment one of them stood less than an inch away from me, the tensed, vibrating back of his knee so close to my face that I could have kissed it by pursing my lips. After a few minutes the three students went thudding back up the stairs, their hollow shouts gradually diminishing.

Sometimes, in a gregarious mood, I climbed Lehman Hall's fire escape and tapped on windows. Often I was told to beat it, but on a few occasions I was invited to climb in over the sill and offered slices of salami and sips of beer. One student opened a can of mandarin orange sections and let me fish them out with my fingers. Another—this is a painful memory—complimented me on my vocabulary. I took this as a signal to draw him into a corner of a stairwell and whisper every dirty word I knew. He listened gravely to my recitation, told me that I had disappointed him seriously, and walked away.

Sometimes I found my way to the college radio station in the bowels of the newly built student union building, waiting politely outside the broadcasting room until the ON THE AIR sign went from red to black. I eased through the door so qui-

etly that it was often a few moments before the announcer—
I remember him: big and prematurely balding, wearing the
Williams uniform of chinos and blue oxford cloth shirt,
loafers, no socks—realized that I was standing behind his
swivel chair. Out! he would mouth at me, making sweeping
motions in the direction of the door, or he would turn to his
microphone, intoning in his loud, round ON THE AIR voice,
Why, it's Miss Bennington again! A few words for the radio
audience, Miss Bennington? What about that hemorrhoid
operation Mr. John Foster Dulles underwent at Bethesda
Naval Hospital this afternoon? Any thoughts on that, Miss
Bennington? Handed the microphone, I spluttered, breathed,
giggled lamely. Not a lot to say, Miss Bennington? I thought
you Bennington girls had an opinion on every subject.

Sometimes I visited the small museum in the lobby of the
redbrick biology building, a few glass cases displaying a tatty
stuffed eagle and a worse-for-wear timber wolf and some
waterlogged organs in jars. It was a chilly, echoing room
with black and white floor tiles and a formaldehyde smell. I
was happy there. If I had timed it right, a certain biology
professor whose name I never learned but whose face I had
judged to be friendly walked through the lobby on his way
out of the building. He knew what I wanted: to be let into
the room with the brain. I followed him down a hall and
waited while he sorted through his keys and unlocked the

door of a small cluttered lab. The fluorescent light flickered on overhead, and I was allowed to stand over the glass vat and stare down at that bleached, puckered thing slowly disintegrating in its murky bath.

Sometimes I walked down Spring Street and stared through the window into the mirrored mahogany gloom of the House of Walsh, watching the salesman as he knelt on a padded footstool, measuring the waists of Williams students. He was an elderly homosexual with a bad toupee—my mother observed that it could be mistaken for a fallen fledgling—who was an object of mockery on the Pine Cobble playground. The House of Walsh was the store where my popular classmates bought their cashmere-blend sweaters and cabled kneesocks. Somewhere I had picked up the idea that it was enemy territory; I think my parents considered it a bastion of anti-Semitism.

Often I dropped in on Bob and Caroline Bahnson, who lived in an apartment at the end of Spring Street in a building with a political history. Two storefronts faced the street, each with a separate entrance. During the Eisenhower-Stevenson campaign they had been used as the headquarters, respectively, of the Democratic and Republican parties. When the Republicans installed a WE LIKE IKE banner across the front of their half of the building, my parents and their friends spent a hilarious evening stenciling and lettering their own banner, designed to read as a continuation of the Republicans'. They hung it under cover of darkness and the next morning a photographer from the *Eagle* was sent to record the result. WE LIKE IKE BUT WE'LL VOTE FOR STEVENSON, the legend read.

The Bahnsons lived in the back of this building, in a cozy warren of overfurnished rooms. Bob Bahnson was an instructor, the most junior member of the economics department. He and Caroline were a kind young couple, still childless. They had met when they both played small parts in a Williamstown summer theater production, and when they first came to dinner at the gray house on College Place, they taught Andy and me to pantomime pulling on the sleeves of a jacket.

Once, when my parents went to see the trotters at Saratoga, I spent the night at the Bahnsons' apartment. I forget exactly when this happened, but I know I was quite young, perhaps four or five—young enough to believe that my parents might win a horse at the racetrack and bring it home in a trailer. Caroline, who was buxom and warm and southern, made a bed for me on the couch, but I was homesick and feverish thoughts of horses were keeping me awake. When she heard me crying she came out of the bedroom in her bathrobe and scooped me up and threw me over her shoulder like a baby. I was already quite big, but that was just what she called me. "Don't cry, baby," she whispered in her soft voice as she paced the living room floor. "You'll see Mama and Daddy in the morning."

Their apartment was generally my last stop; I liked to drop by late in the afternoon, when Bob could be expected to come home from the library for dinner. I sat at the kitchen table drinking cocoa, while Caroline assembled a salad and checked on the progress of their casserole. Sometimes she put me to work chopping vegetables or washing lettuce. We talked only intermittently, but she had a way of making me feel welcome and expected, a small but integral part of their lives.

I divided adults into two camps in those days, those who made conversation by asking about school and those who didn't. Bob and Caroline didn't, and Bob had a particular knack for taking a child seriously, for respectfully soliciting my opinions and hearing me out when I improvised them on the spot. He came bustling into the kitchen, breathing cold and radiating energy, kissed Caroline, poured himself a beer, and sat down to face me across the kitchen table. He asked me what I was reading and solicited my opinions about politics and current events. I knew almost nothing, except that McCarthy was evil and Khrushchev menacing, that Stevenson was intelligent, that Eisenhower was simpleminded and that he looked like a duck (all these views except the last were borrowed from my parents). But Bob Bahnson managed to teach me more than I realized during those talks at his kitchen table. Under his influence I wrote a letter to President Eisenhower about the little black girl who was the first to integrate the public schools in Selma, Alabama, and another to Nikita Khrushchev. This letter is the only sample of my writing that survives my childhood.

College Place
Williamstown, Mass.
Dec. 30, 1957

Dear Mr. Kruschev,

My name is Emily Gordon, I come from a small regural town in New England. I feel that many people in my country are afraid to fight; and even though I am also very afraid of nucleaer war I think that the fear of death and cowardism is my country's main problem.

My family and I all love peace and hate gruesome war. I hope my country and your country do agree to have friendly and lasting pease.

Sincerly Yours,
Emily Gordon (age 10)

Looking at this letter, I'm forced to admit that it's not precocious. If anything, it's a little backward. There are punctuation errors and misspellings—"nucleaer" and "pease" and "sincerly." I'm struck by two other anomalies as well: First, what could I have meant by "regural"? "Regular"? That wouldn't make much sense. Or "regional," perhaps—though that wouldn't, either—or maybe "rural"? Was this one of my combined words? And second, "cowardism": surely a child who had read as much as I should have known the correct form.

So much for the myth that I was a gifted child, or at least a child whose gifts were academically exploitable. I see a Hobbesian glimmer in my speculation about my country's "main problem." This was an incompletely expressed insight into the psychology of the cold war, disguised by an apparent non sequitur: I meant to say that it was my own "cowardism," writ large, that motivated the defensive excesses of the arms race. There's intelligence in this letter, but if it accurately represents my writing at age ten, then my teachers can't be blamed for failing to recognize my superiority.

My visits to the Bahnsons lasted only half an hour or so. The earliest precept my mother succeeded in teaching me was the one against wearing out one's welcome. I knew exactly when to leave: it was when Caroline started tossing the salad. Outside it would be twilight and cold, the western sky pink, the denuded elms black. I would realize how hungry I was and make my way home to College Place.

A Hole
in a Meat

S oon after we moved from the gray house to the white
house, my mother gave a dinner party to celebrate my
father's recent promotion to full professor and his fortieth
birthday. She baked a flag cake—his birthday fell on the
third of July—with blueberry stars and strawberry stripes.
One of his gifts was the book *Life Begins at Forty*; another was
a joke newspaper with a headline announcing his birth in
1917; another was a bottle of pear liqueur containing an actual pear, grossly magnified by the glass. I recall this occasion
so clearly because my upper right front tooth was chipped
when I came through the swinging door between the butler's pantry and the purple dining room and collided with a

platter that my father was carrying away from the table. I remember very precisely his reaction: a head-jerking grimace that was half empathy with my pain, half disgust at my clumsiness.

I suspect that my memories of my parents' faces really begin after the move to the white house. Before that, I remember their smells and voices and hands—one of my father's thumbs had been misaligned by a softball—but when I bring their faces to mind, I realize that I've borrowed the images from photographs. By the time I had matured enough—or just grown tall enough—to record pictures of their faces in my mind, they had begun to age a little; the ligaments around their eyes and mouths had softened enough to allow characteristic expressions to settle in. That grimace of my father's was one of them. Another was a look of blank abstraction, almost a catatonia, that overtook him at odd moments—at the kitchen table, for example, after dinner when he and my mother were drinking their coffee. He was thinking; that was the explanation. And it was true: thinking was my father's gift.

He had been a Jewish golden boy in his youth, slender and blond and Aryan-appearing, the winner of every prize and scholarship. At forty he was an imposing man, balding, with a face like an elongated moon, a Roman nose, and large, contemplative gray eyes. Dead center in his forehead was a perfectly round pearly wart. His waist was beginning to spread, but he was still graceful—lacrosse had been his game as a Rhodes scholar—with long legs and arms that he held slightly flexed at the elbows. He moved, and wore his clothes, with authority; the first time I saw him dressed in black tie and evening slippers, I was shocked by his masculine glamour.

By the time we moved into the white house, I understood that while my father mostly deferred to my mother in aesthetic matters, he had a few tastes and preferences of his own. He liked Braque still lifes, the prose of S. J. Perelman and H. L. Mencken, the movie *The Third Man,* the late Beethoven quartets. Unlike my mother, he responded emotionally to music; as he grew older, this became more important to him. (Was it a solace? My sister, who shares his love of music, suggests that it was.) He had grown up in a nonobservant family and retained only a few shreds of Jewish cultural identity, but he loved rye bread and corned beef and salami, the delicatessen food of his childhood. The unavailability of decent dill pickles in the Berkshires drove him to make his own. Every summer he harvested a crop of Kirby cucumbers from my mother's College Place vegetable garden and soaked them in a brew of brine, spices, dill, and garlic in ceramic crocks in the mudroom. Some of the pickles were removed early; these were the bright green half-sours that still tasted of dill. I liked them best. The others were left to fester, as my father put it, until a skin of ice had settled on the brine, and the pickles were flabby and redolent of garlic. That was the taste and texture that brought back the South Philadelphia childhood he spoke of so rarely.

At one point my father bought an antique printing press. He had been a reporter for the *Philadelphia Inquirer* in his youth and retained a weakness for the paraphernalia of journalism. He kept it in the basement of the white house, next to the shuddering six-armed furnace with a twisted humanoid trunk that made me think of a tormented demigod. He ran off facetious handbills on the printing press and every November he produced cards from my mother's Christmas woodcut in red and green ink. The press was a thing both primitive and ornate, made of black wrought iron, about the size, and roughly the shape, of a Saint Bernard sitting up on its haunches. It was operated by a foot pedal, which caused a squealing wheel to rotate, which in turn caused two thick wooden pallets, one set with type and smeared with ink, the other blank, to slap together resoundingly.

The war between my father and me was waged over the lights I forgot to turn off and the soap I forgot to put back in the soap dish and the tops I forgot to put back on the toothpaste tube. The hectoring and shouting had been going on for years before we moved into the white house. By that time my mother had tried to explain my father and his ways to me. It all had to do, she said, with his childhood in South Philadelphia and the Depression and my grandfather, who had died when I was a baby. I'd seen photographs of this person, short and hefty, with dark evasive eyes, wearing an overcoat and fedora. I'd heard stories about about how he doted on my sister, calling her—this was a relative of mine?—"my princess." Something about his own father (later I learned it was gambling and reckless speculation) left my father chronically anxious about money and drove him to patrol our house incessantly, searching for wastefulnesses to remedy, and also compelled him to make irrational bargain purchases: a lifetime supply of silver polish, for example, when we owned no silver.

My mother explained this in a shrugging, rueful spirit: *tout comprendre c'est tout pardonner.* But I didn't comprehend; she credited me with a sophistication I had yet to develop. We lived in a big house, didn't we? We had food and clothing and comforts. Nobody we knew had ever been dispossessed by poverty. What could it mean, living on College Place, to be put out into the street? To me, my father's obsession with thrift was a mystifyingly simpleminded compulsion, like the fairy-tale giant's grumbling demand for the blood of an Englishman. My sister and brother saw it that way, too, I'm sure, but the difference between them and me was that they adapted their behavior accordingly. They learned to put the soap back in the soap dish and to stay out of his way. I never did.

When he wasn't angry or abstracted, my father was cheerful. He came to the table enthusiastically, stood at his place,

bouncing on his heels and rubbing his palms together in anticipation of the meal. His greeting to me was "Hi, Um!" or
"Hi, Umbly!" How I hated those names, and hated him for
conceiving of them. At the table he often sang a little song:

> I eat my peas with honey.
> I've done it all my life.
> It makes the peas taste funny,
> but it keeps them on the knife.

I hated that, too. He had many other songs, some less objec-
tionable than others, and dozens of jokes, drawn from that
history of his I knew so little about. There were jokes about
chipped beef on toast, about talking dogs in bars, about babies teething on hockey pucks. When he tired of telling
jokes, he told stories from the archive he kept in his head of
the exploits of Hugh Troy, the famous practical jokester
who—for example—rented a concert hall and invited two
sets of guests, one at seven and the other at seven-thirty.
When the second group arrived and were shown to seats in
the balcony, they looked down to see a scatological word
spelled out in bald heads.

All of these jokes and songs and stories were characterized
by a kind of innocent raffishness. They were a standing provo-
cation to my mother, whose background, though equally modest, was more genteel than my father's. She had taken on the

role of unofficial curator of his history, entertaining dinner party guests with the mordant Yiddishisms of his grandmother and colorful bits and pieces extracted from his South Philadelphia childhood. But she never knew quite what to make of the borderline crudeness of his sense of humor. Not that she was offended—the songs and stories were too feeble, really, to have anything but a mildly irritating effect—but she found ways to busy herself so that her back was turned when he brought them out. I took my cue from her: by the time we moved to the white house, I had learned to twist my neck and roll my eyes at the ceiling.

I think my father was sometimes lonely, and a little bewildered, living as he did in a family of which he was the least psychologically sophisticated member. One evening, in an expansive mood at the dinner table, he mentioned that his colleague Lou Behrens had offered us the use of his cabin on an island in Maine for a month. We'd eat very simply: we could catch fish from the lake for our dinners. We'd have to get used to the idea of living together closely and primitively, the way the Behrenses did. There wouldn't be a lot of privacy, my father warned us, adding that the island was so remote that we wouldn't need to wear many clothes. My sister was fifteen at the time, home for Easter vacation from Northfield School for Girls. She stared imploringly at our mother; the plan was never mentioned again.

It would be inaccurate to portray my father as a well-meaning boob. He was often unkind. "Suck in your gut, Em" was his regular remark to me when I presented myself at the breakfast table. At dinner parties he liked to tell a story about my brother's birth: Andy had been such an ugly newborn, the tale went, that the doctor threw him into the slop bucket and swaddled the afterbirth instead. He must have said something along these lines in front of the Barneses, because Jessie once took me aside and explained to me that I wasn't to mind. It was just that my father wasn't very good at understanding people.

So I hated him, or at least I hated him most of the time. Sometimes he confused me by showing a sudden solicitous tenderness. Once I ate a bad hot dog at a picnic and threw up into the Green River. My father was concerned almost to the point of panic; he hovered over me, muttering distracted consolations and squeezing my shoulders as I heaved. And sometimes an observation of mine at the dinner table would turn his head and make his eyes shine. That's *right,* Em, he'd say, bringing his fist down on the table. That's *smart* of you.

I hated my father's attempts to help me with homework. His patience was labored and theatrical, always on the verge of combusting in exasperation. His proximity shut down the higher functions of my brain and sent my thoughts scattering like cockroaches under a strong light. But he surprised me one day when he happened to learn about the Pine Cobble institution of after-school study hall. Apparently it was news to him that I spent hours there nearly every afternoon. He was appalled. "They punish her by making her *study?*" he demanded of my mother.

I took that as a small, thrilling vindication. My mother, with all her enlightened pedagogical notions and for all her concern, had never offered me anything like it. She had been enmired and implicated in my school troubles for years; by the time we moved to the white house, I think she had despaired of any improvement. My father's observation about study hall was hardly subtle or original, but his fresh, rational outrage was my first intimation that his mind was a spacious place, large enough to turn around in. He had always insisted that my own laziness was at the bottom of my academic problems, but, offered evidence that the school had been contributing to them, he revised his view to accommodate it. In the process, he showed that he had not given up hope for me.

My father was far less reasonable than my mother, but his mind could be reached and changed by reason. My mother's mind was a closer, darker, more mysterious place; her opinions were often inflected with irony, but she never changed them, and I never saw the process by which she arrived at them. She asked few questions and was rarely surprised.

———

There was something improvised and a little slapdash about the gray house; rooms had been added to it almost randomly over the years. The white house was more formal and complete, with its high ceilings and mudroom and butler's pantry and three-room attic. But it, too, was full of architectural oddities and hidden places. There was an attic window that looked down into the house rather than out; I liked to station myself behind it to observe my mother as she trudged up the third-floor stairs carrying her sewing basket.

And off the backstairs landing behind my bedroom was a tiny room that I considered my secret. The floor space was no bigger than a double bed, and I stepped down into it as if it were a sunken bathtub. In that room I worked my way through the books on my mother's list. Lying in a litter of army blankets, I made the jump from advanced children's literature to adult books—from *The Secret Garden* to *Mansfield Park*. Later, I smoked the Kents I filched from my mother's purse there. I lit one after another, making myself pleasantly giddy at first and eventually so sick that I had to stagger out to the hall for air. I persuaded myself that I was the only one who knew about that room, but now I realize that of course my mother did, too, and knew all the uses to which I put it.

A Hole in a Meat

In the white house we spread out. Andy had room for his collections of Matchbox toys and model airplanes in his new bedroom, and I was allowed to keep a series of birds in mine. Two were parakeets, the first blue and dropsical, the second a volatile green biter with a talent for escaping from his cage. I worked out a foolproof protocol for capturing him. First, I pulled on my mother's rubber dishwashing gloves and waited for him to light on a flat surface. Then I bunched up the waist of my crinoline petticoat and trapped him under its skirts. Extracting him from this makeshift cage without harming him was the hard part; he struggled desperately in my clumsy gloved hand, twisting his muscular neck and stabbing at the air with his beak. My third and favorite bird was an elegant and mournful-looking black and gray finch. One day as I was admiring him he pitched headfirst off his perch and died. Or rather he died first, I suppose, and then pitched.

James died, too, while we lived in the white house. For weeks he had been morose and snappish, until one day my father took him to the vet and sat with him as he was euthanized. That night we all went to the Walden Theatre to see *Gigi,* the only movie we ever attended as a family. I watched the whole thing—Hermione Gingold and Maurice Chevalier, pink ostrich feathers and gray cobblestones—through a scrim of tears. To this day I hear "Thank Heaven for Little Girls" as a dirge.

Katy went away to boarding school. My father became a consultant to the Ford Foundation and began to travel to New York for a week every month. Eventually he rented a small pied-à-terre apartment on the Upper West Side. I remember our first family visit there, one of two or three we made during the years my father was commuting between Williamstown and Manhattan. We took the train from Hillsdale, New York. I wore white gloves and a costume jewelry bird pin on my coat lapel. Andy wore a bow tie. His cornsilk hair had been slicked back with some kind of pomade. The train was late. My father paced up and down the platform, occasionally flinging a hand toward the sky in exasperation while my mother stood by our baggage smoking a cigarette.

Once in the city, we ate dinner in the restaurant of the midtown hotel where we were staying. This place was another of my father's economies, I suppose. The carpet was gritty and the lights so dim it was hard to read the menu. The room was vast and low-ceilinged and smelled stale. We were served enormous starchy lima beans, which none of us could swallow. Nevertheless, I was enchanted by the louche New York atmosphere of the place, the blinking neon sign outside the window, and the row of patrons sitting shoulder to shoulder at the bar. I had been listening to *Guys and Dolls* on the record player at home and I took these characters to be Damon Runyon–style gangsters.

The next day we attended a birthday party for a Ford

Foundation child in Central Park. We ate roasted chestnuts and rode the carousel, then returned to the birthday child's apartment on Central Park West. This was a birthday party like none I'd ever attended. More adults than children were present, all of them apparently hell-bent on giving us a good time. Some adult played the piano and we sang along; cake was served, and I was congratulated for being a member of the clean-plate club.

Suddenly and unaccountably, the hostess—the birthday child's mother—burst into tears. Her face crumpled and she sank to her knees as though she had been hit with a poison dart. Other grown-ups surrounded her in a tight circle, blocking our view. They half lifted her out of the room into the kitchen, where we could hear her sobs over the jolly banging of the piano. Eventually my mother emerged and retrieved our coats. We were handed our party-favor bags as we filed out the door. Years later, my mother explained that the husband of the hostess had left her for another woman the night before the birthday party.

Then we were on the street once again, headed back to the park to visit the zoo for a few hours, then on to upper Broadway to meet my father for dinner at Prexy's ("the hamburger with a college education"). My parents sat in a booth, but Andy and I took seats at the counter, where we made the acquaintance of an elderly European with an astrakhan hat and an apparently unfeigned curiosity about children. We told him about the death of James, our absent older sister, our house. "You are the youngest?" he asked Andy, "and your sister who is not with us is the eldest?" Andy nodded. The man turned to me. "So you are the one in the middle?" I nodded. "Then *you*," he said, looking me dead in the eye, "are the ham in the sandwich."

———

Once, when I was in my thirties, I babysat for the young son and daughter of a new colleague of my husband. This man had just moved a long distance to take a job in my husband's department, expecting his wife to join him. Without warning, she backed out of the marriage and returned to her parents in Japan. The little girl, who was five or six, told me about a dream she'd had the previous night. In this dream she watched her father through what she called a "hole in a meat." She saw him running back and forth "like a crazy man"—first one way and then the other.

I was puzzled: "A hole in a meat?" I asked. "You know," she said, "like a meat in a cartoon," and after a moment I understood. She had dreamed that she was watching her father through the aperture provided by the hollow marrow bone in a stylized steak or chop—the kind that scheming cartoon cats dangle in front of the noses of stupid cartoon dogs. It took me a day or two to appreciate the metaphorical cunning of her dreaming mind: this tiny view of her frantic father—running first one way and then the other —was a perfect representation of a child's necessarily limited perspective.

Around the time when my father began his Ford Foundation consultancy, my view of my mother was cropped in a similar way. I saw her, for example, sitting calmly upright in bed, a book in her hand, smiling and nodding at my brother and me as we closed the door to her bedroom. Inexplicably, it was the middle of the afternoon. Andy and I had no idea why she had taken to getting in bed at this hour. We simply accepted this new habit of hers without question, though we found it inconvenient to be asked to contain our disputes and demands for two full hours every afternoon.

It was my impression that my mother had read every novel that had been written in the past and that all that remained to her were contemporary ones by writers like Peter De Vries and James Gould Cozzens. When she climbed the stairs to her bedroom in the afternoon, carrying a glass of iced coffee in one hand and her mending in the other, she tucked one of these big glossy books from the "current reading" shelf at the public library under her arm. Andy and I were invited to watch her take off and fold her slacks and to help her pull the covers over her legs. She settled into bed, propped up in her corduroy bed chair. (I was fascinated by this object she used so intimately, this drastically incomplete little man whose only job was to embrace.) Then we were expected to leave. One day when she was resting, we both came barreling up the stairs, howling and weeping and demanding that she intervene in our fight. My father stepped out of his study, grabbed us by our upper arms, pulled us down the stairs and into the family room. He closed the double doors behind him, squatted down, and engaged our eyes. "You children," he said in a level voice, "are *killing* your mother."

Killing? Andy and I clutched each other and wailed in unison. It's not too late, said our father. You can help. You can stop fighting. You can make your own beds. You can keep your rooms tidy. You can set the table and sweep the floor.

—

I believe I was eight when my father said this, or seven going on eight. By now I was in trouble at Pine Cobble, failing in Arithmetic. I wasn't yet the full-blown schoolyard pariah I would become in a year or so, but I no longer received any birthday party invitations that weren't extended to the entire class. I spent my recesses on a swing set in a far corner of the playground; for some reason it was one that other children rarely used.

Around this time I had an uncanny nightmare, one of those potent ones that holds a charge of incommunicable dread for years. In the dream I found myself inside what I took at first to be a faintly lit cavern but which, I somehow came to understand, was actually the gutted body cavity of a long-dead mastodon. Rearing up in the vaulted gloom of this interior space were towering structures, great brooms and fans and harps formed of strings of bone or tendon that stretched from the floor of the beast's belly to its high, shadowy ribs. The air of the dream was heavy and smelled of the ether-saturated gauze pad that had been clamped over my nose when my adenoids were removed.

That dream, as I recall it, ushered in a new era in the development of my consciousness. I had reached the age of explanation, and perhaps in a fumbling effort to identify a cause for the troubles in my life, I became convinced that something was medically wrong with me. I pictured this malady or defect as a soft discolored area like a bruise on a peach, slowly spreading under the skin of my belly, not yet visible but soon to manifest itself. I never spoke of my fear to anyone, and it was greatly exacerbated when my mother—for reasons she never explained—began taking me to doctors. We started by visiting our family physician, the doctor who took care of every faculty child I knew. This was the first time I had ever been to his office when I was apparently well, without so much as a booster shot to serve as pretext. I trusted Dr. Steinglass, but when my mother and I were ushered into his Spring Street consulting room I was in a state of speechless, dry-mouthed panic, terrified that my bad spot would be discovered.

Dr. Steinglass took my wrist between his thumb and forefinger and drew back in feigned alarm at my rapid pulse. He rested his hand on my shoulder and waited for a moment before he began his methodical examination. He measured my blood pressure, weighed me, tested my reflexes, peered into my eyes, ears, and throat with a tiny flashlight. Then he hoisted me up onto his examining table and palpated my abdomen with gentle, insistent fingers. All the while he hummed: I imagine now it was a snatch of lied. In my panic and incipient relief I giggled, but Dr. Steinglass took that to be ticklishness and made a comic face at me. He pulled a sheet up over my exposed stomach to signal that the examination was concluded. "She is very well indeed," he announced in his German-accented basso profundo. My mother had been sitting on a child-size chair in a corner of his office. "Very well nourished," he added.

Joseph Steinglass and his wife Clara had fled Hitler's Germany. The Women's Exhange consignment shop, where my mother and other faculty wives volunteered as a pricer, had sponsored them and helped establish him in his practice. He was jovial and avuncular: "Is she always such a chatterbox?" he asked my mother when I was five and feverish. Every faculty child knew the sound of his steady tread on the stairs and recognized the reverberations of his voice, which could set the water in a bedside glass quivering before he entered the room. Every child had been invited to pull open the accordionated mouth of his black leather doctor's bag, a gift from the local Visiting Nurse Association, and search for a lollipop at the end of his visit.

He was a beloved figure in Williamstown, but even so, my mother was apparently unsatisfied with the results of his examination. She took me to the other doctor in Williamstown. I knew better than to ask why: my mother was the parent who explained the world to me, but if she had chosen to stay silent on a certain subject, my questions would cause her to stiffen and withdraw.

Dr. Feeney had come to Williamstown from the north of England, a refugee from socialized medicine. He supplemented his income by running a motel on the outskirts of town. His daughter Sheila was two grades ahead of me at Pine Cobble, a celebrated field hockey fullback with chapped knees and a ferocious squint. Dr. Feeney was tall and slightly stooped, with ruddy cheeks and a coarse thatch of hair that was either prematurely white or unnaturally blond. He had a way of pausing abruptly in midsentence, as though he had just that moment remembered something that puzzled and confounded him. He was not approved of by the Williamstown faculty wives; in fact he was considered a crank, but he was more up-to-date in his views than Dr. Steinglass, who believed that obesity in a child was something to be prized. He weighed me and gave a cursory examination—inveighing all the while against socialized medicine—and prescribed some capsules I was to swallow before meals. "They should cut down the intake," he promised, and for a while they did, filling my stomach with sulfurous bubbles that backed up my throat and burst against my palate.

Some weeks after our visit to Dr. Feeney, my mother and I drove in silence to North Adams State Teachers College, where I was tested by a man I now assume was an educational psychologist. My mother and my doctors had apparently fallen back on an old hypothesis: the problem was in my brain.

The psychologist's tie was yellow and his pants were too short. He wore patent leather shoes and argyle socks. He had parted his hair just above one ear and combed it all the way across his bald pate in stripes. His hands were spotty, and trembled. The session began with an abbreviated game of checkers which I was allowed to win. Then I was asked to move to a table under a panel of fluorescent lamps, next to a single window looking out on a sidewalk and a patch of snowy hillside. (My mother walked by twice, her chin tucked into the collar of her coat, a cigarette in her hand, trailing smoke.) A small pile of booklets appeared on the table and I understood what I'd been brought to this office for. Early in the testing, I recognized some items from the examination

I'd been given by Dorothy Barnes. There would be no walking out of this one. I was older now, and couldn't pretend I didn't know better. My mother was on patrol outside. But the real reason I stayed and completed the testing was that I felt sorry for the psychologist, who sat all day in this grim little office playing board games with children and asking them questions about their pets. Most of his testing subjects, I imagined, must have been underprivileged students from the North Adams public schools. How often had it happened that a child whose father was a professor at Williams sat at this table? It was no wonder, I thought, that he seemed so eager to make me feel welcome.

He was solicitous of my comfort from the moment I came into the room, offering me apple juice and vanilla cookies. I accepted the juice but declined the cookies, as I knew my mother would have wished. But half an hour later, when I was struggling to replicate a pattern in the testing booklet with a set of six red and white blocks, I worked up the courage to clear my throat and ask if maybe I couldn't have a few of those cookies after all.

Of course! Of course! The psychologist leaped to his feet. He returned with another glass of juice and a saucer on which he had placed three of the vanilla wafers I'd been offered originally and three chocolate marshmallow cookies as well, wrapped diagonally in a paper napkin. It passed through my mind for an instant that the cookies might somehow be part of the test. I looked up at the psychologist and he nodded reassuringly. "Why don't we take a little break?" he suggested. I ate two cookies, then three. After a brief pause I ate the last one. The psychologist glanced at his watch and shrugged. He gave me a sad little smile, as if to let me know that it pained him to remind me that all he could offer was a temporary reprieve.

The results of that testing session appeared some weeks later in a blue cardboard binder in a drawer in my mother's desk. I was able to take a quick look at its contents; I remember seeing the words "anxiety neurosis" and pages of baffling columns of numbers. That folder followed me. I saw it when I was sixteen, propped on the crossed knee of a new therapist as he interviewed me, and again at eighteen, resting on the desk of the psychologist who administered a new battery of psychological tests to me when I was admitted to The Austen Riggs Center.

—

My parents had always entertained, but the parties they held in the gray house had been big and casual, with a residue of graduate-student raucousness. They began with noisy, protracted, hilarious cocktail hours, the guests all jammed into the less formal of the two small living rooms. Late in the evening, my mother served a buffet supper in the dining room. Guests took their plates and wineglasses and distributed themselves around the house in clusters on the porch or in my father's study, or in pairs at the table in the kitchen where Andy and I were fed our breakfasts. I remember coming to the head of the stairs in my pajamas during one of these parties—I must have been three or four—and finding a clutch of young faculty couples sitting on the steps, balancing plates of my mother's choucroute garnie on their laps. I announced that God had come out from behind a cloud and talked to me through the window in my bedroom. (At that age I was preoccupied with God and Jesus, an embarrassment to my agnostic parents.) I remember the explosion of laughter, the adoring smiles, the arms reaching out to embrace me, my giddy puzzled delight.

After my father began to commute to New York, my parents' entertaining style changed. They continued to give large cocktail parties—my father called them "cocktail bashes"— where elaborate hors d'oeuvres were served, but now their dinner parties were smaller, more formal sit-down affairs with several courses. The guests included senior faculty members now, and sometimes judges and local politicians. James Finney Baxter, the one-lunged blowhard president of the college, sat at my parents' table, sometimes accompanied by his chatty secretary Fay, who taught me to cross my legs and cradle a glass in a cocktail napkin. My mother had become a

skillful hostess. My father presided over the table with authority, telling anecdotes in his booming voice, pronouncing
judgments on his colleagues: "talented but unsound," "still a
little wet behind the ears," "appalling, just appalling."

My mother had been known for her dashing, if simplified, French-influenced menus. In the white house she became a serious cook. She spent days in the kitchen before a
dinner party chopping and grating vegetables and whipping
egg whites to stiff peaks. Somehow she acquired a miniature
blowtorch that she used to caramelize the surfaces of the
individual crème brûlées she served in shallow terra-cotta
ramekins. She served quiche—then called quiche Lorraine—
at a dinner party in 1958, a full ten years before it became
fashionable.

Andy and I were banished from the table in the purple dining room, but we took every chance we got to peek
through the swinging butler's pantry door at the assembled
company. My mother's cheeks, which had looked pale in the
wintry light of the kitchen that afternoon, shone rosily in
the candlelight as she moved around the table serving the
first course. She was graceful in her sleeveless black silk
moiré sheath, which I'd seen pinned to patterns on the floor
of her sewing room the day before and displayed on her
dressmaker's dummy that very morning, its hem still basted
with white thread. (How that headless, legless thing dis-
turbed me, with its narrow waist and militant bosom.)

A Hole in a Meat

By the time the marinated shrimp had been admired and eaten and cleared away, my mother was emitting a steady glow. She tilted her head a little roguishly to murmur something into the ear of her dinner partner. My father walked around the table, refilling wineglasses, resting a confident hand on a shoulder here, leaning down to catch a remark there. My mother spoke—Andy and I couldn't quite hear what she said—and a general swell of laughter rose. All through the meal it rolled in like surf, and if we peeked through the pantry door just as the laughter crested, we were sometimes rewarded with the sight of her special ecstatic smile, a quick toss of the chin and a flashing contraction of the facial muscles that lit the room like summer lightning.

The mother of the morning after was utterly unlike the mother of the night before. I'd find her hunched over her coffee at the kitchen table, smoking steadily and coughing, answering my questions with monosyllables, steeling herself for the day's chores. On the morning after a dinner party, dressed in the clothes she wore for everyday chores, she looked somehow more like a tough little boy than a grown woman. (In fact, she had been mistaken for one repeatedly by a nearsighted great-aunt who lived with the Barneses for a while. "Oh, little boy," she called from her window, waving a five-dollar bill as my mother passed, "will you run me an errand?") Nobody would take this shrunken androgyne for the hostess who had sat bare-armed and smiling in candlelight eight hours earlier. Looking through the hole in a meat of my childhood, I could not reconcile the two, just as I could not put together the sunny mother of my early childhood with the mother I had heard—on two or three occasions—weeping behind the closed door of her bedroom.

She was the one who was ill, I concluded, not me. She was dying of cancer. I gathered support for my diagnosis in the visits she had begun to pay to her own doctor at the Williams infirmary. I found evidence in her pallor, her cough, her naps, her lack of appetite and loss of weight. (For most of the day she subsisted on iced coffee and Kents. Dinner was her only substantial meal. In later years, dinner was more or less eliminated as well.) I overheard certain remarks: on the phone she mentioned that Dr. Driscoll had suggested that "the floor might need shoring up." This brought to mind a notion of internal dissolution and collapse that was no less horrible for being unvisualizably vague. Once I heard my father ask, "What did Dr. Driscoll say?" My mother answered, "Oh, the usual. Take aspirin. Pull up my socks." I took this to mean that her cancer was of long standing and too advanced for anything but palliative treatment (the aspirin). Dr. Driscoll—a poker-faced stoic himself—had told her to accept the inevitable.

I knew this was the way it sometimes happened because I had eavesdropped on a hushed discussion at the Women's

Exchange between my mother and several other faculty wives doing inventory in the back room. I had learned other horrors in the school of these conversations—once I heard the wives whispering about a baby born without eyes—but the information I picked up from the discussion about Mrs. Bourse stayed with me for years. She was the wife of a history professor, the mother of one of my classmates at Pine Cobble, and she had been told she had cancer and was going to die in less than a year. The Bourses had decided to go on a walking tour of England, the wives said, while she was still well.

While she was still well? A mortally ill woman could walk through England, still well and dying all the while? I knew, of course, about the kind of illness that put you in bed with a fever, and I knew about sudden catastrophes like heart attacks and strokes that made people clutch their chests or heads and fall to the ground. I knew that people died, of course, but before I overheard the conversation about Mrs. Bourse I had never considered the idea that they might live in full consciousness that they were dying. Or rather, I had, but only for long enough to blink it away, like an ash in my eye. Did growing up mean that I might have to know about my own dying? Too hard! The special practices of adulthood— smoking and drinking coffee and alcohol, which were then so nearly universal that I assumed I would take them up the moment I got the chance (and I did)—were not just privileges, I realized. They were consolations.

At Pine Cobble we happened to be studying tumors in biology class. My textbook showed a photograph of a cross section of one, which I remember as a smooth thing with a kind of shimmering watermark on its surface and a gelatinous border, like a slice of my mother's chicken liver pâté. In class I kept my thumb hooked under that page, flipping it up and glancing at the image furtively every few minutes to inoculate myself against the fearfulness of the image. My biology teacher, the ugly, charismatic Mr. Yaple, who might have taught me a thing or two even if I hadn't been motivated by my obsession, seemed heartened and surprised by my sudden interest in the difference between normal cell division and metastasis. For a few weeks my quizzes came back with gold stars. With his brisk, clinical treatment of the subject, Mr. Yaple legitimated my fascination with cancer and braced me against my fear of it. Then we moved on to disorders of the circulatory system and the horror returned with a new virulence, stronger for all I had learned and could not now forget.

About everything I experienced or remembered or encountered I asked myself the question: does this have to do with cancer? In those days there seemed to be a lot that did. There was the issuing of the surgeon general's report, which caused my father to give up cigarettes for a few weeks and my mother to smoke hers in my bathroom until he relapsed. There was fallout, and strontium 90 in our milk. There was the Quaker summer camp where Andy and I had been sent for six weeks one summer, where we watched films showing blackened fissures on the napes of the slender necks of survivors of Hiroshima and Nagasaki and listened to lectures about the projected incidence of cancers at varying distances from the blast site of a nuclear explosion. (Andy and I were nine and ten at the time, and suffered nightmares.) There was the novel *On the Beach* by Nevil Shute, which my mother brought home from the current reading shelf at the library. I followed the book as she moved it around the house and managed to read most of it in quick furtive sessions while she was out of the room. What I remember still has the power to raise the hair on my arms: after nuclear war, a couple living on the coast of Australia awaits death from radiation sickness (cancer, by my reckoning then, or close enough to it). The rest of the world is dead or dying, and death will come to them from halfway across the globe, blown by the prevailing winds. Prevailing winds: what a beautiful and terrible pairing of words. In *On the Beach,* everyone living will die within weeks, and knows it. Everyone is Mrs. Bourse.

My obsession was carried by the prevailing winds of the late nineteen fifties, the ambient fears of annihilation and mutation at large in the world. But even in the absence of this influence I feel sure now that I would have developed my conviction that my mother had cancer. It was overdetermined, because in my mind this cancer of hers was inextricably bound up with her womanliness. Though I never quite guessed at the anatomical location of the malignancy—by now it had probably spread everywhere, even to her heart—I knew its origin was gynecological.

Her cancer had something to do (here my theory utterly lost coherence and plausibility) with the mulberry color of her nipples, which I had seen when I visited her in her bath. It had to do with the sucking action of the bathwater as she hoisted herself out of it, the way it pulled her breasts into pendulous dugs, like the ones that hung from the chests of stooping African women in *National Geographic,* and the contrast between these soft appendages and her jutting pelvic bones. It had to do with the nests of varicose veins behind her knees, and with certain smells my sensitive young nose had detected. Or perhaps I imagined them, having overheard my mother warn my sister that a menstruating woman who failed to keep herself scrupulously clean risked smelling "like a monkey house."

The body rising up out of the bathwater was a thing of amazing plasticity. Shrouded in a sweater on a winter morning it was concave and hollow, folded in on itself like a praying mantis; in a cocktail dress, molded by a bra and girdle, it was voluptuously convex, aggressively feminine. My mother's nudity was so full of change and possibility, so unlike my own featureless pudginess. I found it hard to believe that I would ever grow into a woman like her.

There had been, and was, so much going on in the small theater of her body: pregnancy and childbirth and lactation and menstruation. Her body was mutability itself, and in my mind it was a short step from mutability to mutation. She was forty now, and if her confused, exhausted cells had stayed at their posts all these years and refused to mutiny, that could only have been the kind of miracle that people like my parents no longer thought possible.

—

Whenever my mother left the house wearing her Peck & Peck tweed skirt with stockings and her low-heeled black pumps, I knew she was on her way to one of her appointments with her own doctor, the director of the Williams College infirmary. One day I watched from the living room window as she climbed into the Plymouth station wagon, pulled out of the driveway, and headed down the road between the Haystack Monument and the town cemetery. I waited a few minutes to give her time to arrive and climb the stairs to Dr. Driscoll's office. Then I jumped on my bike and took a jolting shortcut down a path through a sloping meadow to the parking area behind the redbrick infirmary. I flattened myself and my bike in long grass and waited. From this vantage point I knew I would have a clear view of her face when she emerged from the building. Her expression would tell me how it stood.

After a time, the back door opened. My mother appeared with Dr. Driscoll and they talked for a few moments, framed by the dark green clinic door. I saw right away that there was nothing grave or significant or even particularly intimate about their conversation. They were chatting socially, just as they might have done at one of my parents' cocktail parties. They laughed together once. Dr. Driscoll glanced at his watch and raised his palms in the universal gesture of regret and apology. My mother turned to walk the short distance across the gravel to the Plymouth station wagon, her face still lit with social animation. She rummaged in her purse for her car keys, and as she drove away I saw that her expression had reverted to a composed neutrality.

She did not have cancer, and I was bitterly disappointed. She had slipped out of the net of the drama I had prepared for her and reestablished herself in the ordinary world of car keys and conversations. Watching her chat with Dr. Driscoll, it seemed that nothing had ever been wrong: no deep sighs, no hunched shoulders at the breakfast table, no coughing, no silences in the car on the way to North Adams. All through my childhood and adolescence she did this: just at the moment when the sighs and the silences seemed to have reached a point of critical mass, she would square her shoulders and stub out her cigarette. "I must get on my horse," she would declare, and sighing deeply once again, she would rise to her feet.

What had I hoped for from this cancer I'd given her? A fantasy of tearful disclosure—I'd force it out of her if necessary—and restored intimacy, I suppose. A charmed interval before her death and after it an opportunity to mourn and celebrate her memory. I was already composing the eulogy in my imagination. "My mother," it began, "was a very unusual woman. . . ." There was something else at work as well. I couldn't have articulated it then and I'm not sure I can now. All I can say is that it's the same thing that makes my heart lift when I see BREAKING NEWS scroll across the TV screen. All my life I've been subject to this shameful thrill at the prospect of calamity, this wish that the world might come apart so that at last I could see what had been hidden by the wholeness of things.

By the Sea

My summer life was radically simple and free. I rose at dawn, pulled on shorts and a T-shirt, ate my oatmeal and drank my orange juice and left the house. I cut across the campus, a feminine place now, leafy and quiet with the students gone, and walked through a stand of mannerly pines past the Haystack Monument and on into a meadow that Buildings and Grounds allowed to run riot with Queen Anne's lace and Indian paintbrush. I liked to linger there for a while, especially during the weeks in August when I could part the long grass and discover colonies of wild strawberries growing close to the ground in whorled nests of mottled leaves.

I continued past the infirmary and the meadow beyond it. Even dogs with good addresses ran wild in the Williamstown summers, and often a pack of them would surround me, yelping and jumping and jamming their noses into my crotch. I knew several of these dogs by name and shouted at them for forgetting themselves. With my mismatched clothes and snarled hair I must have looked like a Dickensian ragamuffin, but in the middle years of the 1950s nobody in Williamstown gave a second thought to a scruffy little girl walking barefoot on a summer morning.

My destination was always the McDougals' house. Duncan and Stuart McDougal were faculty brats like me, sons of John McDougal, a political scientist and historical biographer. We three and Tom Sommers, the only townie in our group, had been summer friends since we were all six or seven. From the moment the four of us found one another we wrapped ourselves in an impenetrable cocoon of collaborative fantasy.

All of us went to Pine Cobble, but we barely acknowledged one another at school. To put it more accurately, Duncan and Stuart and Tom barely acknowledged me. Neither Duncan nor Tom had any popularity to spare: Stuart was respected at school, but he was a marginal member of our group, included mostly because he was Duncan's brother. They knew better than to risk what little they had by associating with me. Even so, outside of school I was given an equitable share of power by the others—perhaps more than that in later years, when I learned to play up the novelty of my gender, to make a mystery of it. Tom, especially, was susceptible to that.

Duncan was a grubby, red-cheeked fat boy, even fatter and grubbier than I, forever wiping his steamy glasses with the tail of his shirt and applying ChapStick to his lips. He was self-possessed and sensible and probably the brightest student at Pine Cobble. When I last heard news of him—this was thirty years ago, at least—he was living in Scotland, an acolyte of R. D. Laing. Stuart was redheaded and fox-faced, very different from his guileless brother. I have no idea what he grew up to be, but I can picture him as a Machiavellian political adviser or a shadowy second in command.

Tom's father worked at the Cornish Wire factory on the way to North Adams and his mother did tutoring at home for the public school. The Sommerses lived in a small blue box of a house in a new development a distance from the campus. An unconscious snob, I looked down on them. Tom was a sensitive, moody boy, a natural draftsman and a budding autodidact. He moved from one historical enthusiasm to another—Norse mythology, the Indians of the Great Plains, the origins of the Nazi Party—and spent hours reading in the library stacks.

Now I realize that Tom was quite handsome, though I wouldn't have characterized him that way then. He had a

long, serious, rosy face and smoky blue eyes with dark girl-
ish lashes. He was the first of a line of boys whose ardent,
earnest, wooden masculinity brought out an oblique, feminine, slightly catty side of my nature I was always surprised
to discover.

—

At the beginning of my association with Duncan and Stuart
and Tom, I remember the Time Machine stories. We sat on
the sagging steps of the McDougals' porch at the feet of Jack
McDougal and listened to tales of adventure set in different
historical periods. Andy often joined us for these sessions,
though it was clear from the beginning that he was not a full-
time member of our group. A neighbor girl sometimes sat in
as well, until Stuart and Duncan and I discouraged her attendance by tying her to a tree and tossing lighted matches at her.
Each story allowed a different child to assume a starring role:
Duncan was Benjamin Franklin's nephew, for example, accompanying his uncle on kite-flying expeditions. I was a hand-
maiden to Cleopatra, rubbing the feet of my mistress with
fragrant oils as we were borne down the Nile on an orna-
mented barge. These stories provided me with the only out-
line of history that I ever managed to internalize. They were
highly colored and simplified and personalized and lodged in
my memory like nothing I was taught in school.

And so did the image of Jack McDougal as he told them. He sat in shorts on a folded towel on a peeling wooden deck chair gazing out over his overgrown lawn, holding one or both of Duncan and Stuart's two toddler sisters on his lap, his long hairy legs extended, his head thrown back, one arm flung out in the direction of the child featured in that afternoon's story—"and then our own STUART found himself at the mercy of a RAVENING MOB"—his tenor voice rising to a strained bellow or falling to a hoarse whisper. He was a tall, balding, awkward man with a mobile rosebud mouth and a perpetually sunburnt bulbous nose. His pronunciation was buoyantly clipped, like FDR's, and his energy was prodigious.

———

Standards of cleanliness varied widely in the faculty households where I spent time as a child. The Barneses' house was perhaps the cleanest, because Jessie had daily help and was a skilled delegator: she never hesitated to call down from her bedroom and order any child who happened into her house to sweep the kitchen floor or polish the silver. My own mother kept our houses reasonably tidy and running smoothly with very little outside help; it was important to her to seem relaxed about housekeeping, but the burdensome notions her own mother had instilled in her about airing rooms and turning over mattresses kept her perpetually exhausted. Her standards grew higher in later years, when my father became a full professor and our family could afford the services of Carla, the first black person I ever knew, on more than an occasional basis.

The McDougals lived at the end of a street that began at the heart of the campus and petered out into a winding-dirt-road wilderness we called "Indian Country." The house was a squat, brown-shingled Cape, set far back from the road on a choppy, hummocked lawn. At the front of the yard was a great pine tree with an underskirt of heavy branches, a natural fort where Duncan and Stuart and Tom and I met to conduct our business and plan our activities. At the side was a scruffy vegetable garden, maintained by Jack McDougal. At the back was a path cutting through a dense growth of blackberry bushes to a semi-derelict garage where Duncan left bottles of cider to harden. At the edge of the driveway was a little wooded rise that I remember clearly for unremembered reasons, and a tumbledown wooden latticed structure that I believe was once a kind of arbor.

The house was a fertile academic chaos, full of books and musical instruments and piles of unfolded laundry. The purpose of many of the rooms had become blurred by the time I got to know Duncan and Stuart; the dining room had been overlaid with a music room that was in the process of becoming an all-purpose storage area, as was the mostly unused living room, where the overflow of a large library was stacked high against the walls and the small toys of the tiny McDougal daughters crackled underfoot. There was more unoccupied space in that room than anywhere else in the house; Duncan and I once used a vacuum cleaner to blow up a giant Army surplus weather balloon there. We had ordered it from the back pages of a Superman comic book and waited eight weeks for delivery. Fully inflated, it pressed against two walls and bulged out the doorway.

Jack McDougal's upstairs study was the only tidy place in the house. Surrounded by stacks of index cards bound in stout rubber bands, he pounded out page after page of biography in that monkish little room on an Olympia typewriter. My own father's study was a place for talk. Jack McDougal's study was a writer's lair and it smelled of sweat: not the rounded stench of bodily exertion that I knew from the college gym on Spring Street but the sharp reek of hard thinking.

Whenever I remember Jack McDougal's study, I always and inexplicably bring to mind an exotically embroidered length of dark red fabric. This was something I never actually saw at the McDougals' house or anywhere else, though I may have borrowed it from an illustration in my copy of the *Arabian Nights*. Those two images—that austere, orderly, functional room reserved for writing somehow juxtaposed with that billowing apparition glinting with gold threads— chime together in my mind with a familiar and cherished dissonance.

—

After a few summers the Time Machine stories ended—I don't remember why. Perhaps Jack McDougal ran out of material, or decided we were too old. By that time we no longer needed the glue of narrative to keep our group together. As the summers went by I spent more and more time at the McDougals' house until I found myself more or less living there, sleeping in Duncan and Stuart's spectacularly messy room on a cot next to their bunk bed. In the McDougals' house all the windows were left open all night (except for the one in the study), letting in gusts of wind and puffs of rain and Duncan's two fat tabbies, which padded in and out at will, dropping maimed field mice behind the radiator and using my stomach as a springboard to reach their master in the upper bunk.

Duncan and I talked as we lay in the dark. (Stuart kept his own counsel, and fell asleep instantly.) Once he asked me why I did so badly in school. Put so straightforwardly, this question startled me; nobody had ever asked it before. I answered that I didn't know, which was the truth, and asked Duncan how it was that he did so well. He paused, considered and gave me the same answer I had given him: I don't know. Then he added that he liked to study, liked to do what he was good at. That was the end of that conversation, which

I've never forgotten. Friendship licensed him to ask a question that would have angered or shamed me coming from someone else. It had the effect of shifting—slightly, but significantly— the arrangement of the contents of my mind. For years, my school failure had been resting at the center of my life like a flat-bottomed rock. Duncan's inquiry had the effect of tipping it up a little, just enough so that I could catch a glimpse of its underside.

Duncan's mother was rarely up before ten. She was Meg (like many faculty children, I called most of the parents of my friends by their first names), dark-haired, blue-eyed, and bosomy, some years younger than Jack, with a ripe Celtic prettiness that turned blowsy over the years I knew her. Her face, now that I recall it, was a delicate version of Duncan's; she had the same fleshy nostrils and full cheeks, but hers were a glowing pink rather than a mottled red. She had a slow-blooming, relishing smile, often directed at nobody in particular. There was something off-kilter about her emotions; often she treated me with sugary solicitude, only to turn and snap at me a moment later. I was afraid of her, glad to be out of the house before she came drifting down the stairs in her white kimono, her two tangle-headed daughters following like a retinue.

As far as I could tell, Meg did very little around the house. The McDougals had a housekeeper, stout, middle-aged, dirty-minded Mrs. Smithers. She didn't seem to do much housework, either; we usually found her at the kitchen table, smoking Parliaments and muttering insinuations about what she guessed the boys were getting up to with me at night. Occasionally I saw her ironing. There was no breakfast to sit down to; Mrs. Smithers waved us to the pantry, where we foraged for graham crackers and peanut butter.

We spent the days roaming, going farther afield and moving faster than I ever had as a solitary wanderer. We gathered up Tom at his house—he was rarely allowed to spend the night at Duncan's—and struck out for Indian Country, or beyond that to New Inverness. On very hot days we rode our bikes out Route Seven to Sand Springs, a public swimming pool attached to a small soft-drink bottling company. To get to the pool, we walked through the cool dark warehouse past shelves loaded with bottles of grape and orange and cherry and lemon soda, all glowing like stained glass. I have intensely happy memories of that pool. The soda was so cheap as to be nearly free. I was not allowed to drink it at home; at Sand Springs I guzzled all I could hold. I loved the shade-dappled water, littered with leaves from an overhanging linden tree. I performed one perfectly executed underwater somersault after another, working my way up to six in a row one summer. Sand Springs was frequented by anonymous townies: Pine Cobble students went elsewhere to swim. I was still too young to feel self-conscious in a bathing suit.

By the Sea

One summer a girl tried to befriend me at Sand Springs. I forget her name. She was a few years older, tall and thick-bodied, with widely spaced protuberant blue eyes. She had been left in charge of three younger siblings, whom she ignored. One day she and I rose to the surface simultaneously and found ourselves face-to-face. Without introduction, she offered to paint my toenails, bringing a foot to the surface and flexing it to display her own toes, done in frosted apricot. We climbed out of the pool and sat down in the grass. She reached into her straw carryall and pulled out a dozen pots of nail polish, one at a time, inviting me to consider each color. I eliminated red and pearl white and shocking pink right away, dwelled for a while on metallic blue and pumpkin and settled on a soft shade of apple green. Just as she was separating my toes with wads of tissue paper, Duncan hauled himself out of the pool at the deep end and lumbered over to stand above us, sheets of water cascading down his belly and thighs. He was still wearing his nose plugs and flippers. "Time to go," he said.

On cool days we climbed Stone Hill, a real hike, beginning in a high alpine pasture studded with cow pies and proceeding up a steep wooded trail to the rocky summit, where the four of us sat panting on a bench carved from stone. When we returned to Duncan's empty house in the middle of the afternoon we were desperately hungry and stuffed ourselves with whatever we could find. Sometimes we poured a box of Wheaties into a large aluminum mixing bowl, doused it with milk and sugar, and ate it communally with soupspoons.

—

By the time Duncan and Tom and I were nine and Stuart was eight, the era of freestyle wandering had ended. We institutionalized our association by creating an interlocking set of secret societies, each of us serving as president of one and secretary or treasurer or sergeant at arms of each of the others. We met under the skirts of the great pine on the McDougals' lawn, or in the basement where Duncan kept his reeking chemistry set, or sometimes at my house, in a narrow storage room with a nearly invisible door off the hall that led to the porch.

Stuart's club was the Fighting Star, with a mission to overthrow Williamstown bullies. We drew up step-by-step overthrow plans—illustrated by Tom with stick-figure drawings, some intact, some exploding—but we never reached the stage of implementation. The Fighting Star was a lesson to us all in the way organizations tend to paralyze action. Tom's club was the Move for Indians. He passed on to us the lore he learned from the hours he spent reading in the library and collected a quarter every month from each of us to send to Indian reservations. Mine was the short-lived Cross-legged Clan, which had no particular purpose, though when we met I insisted that we all sit cross-legged in a circle. This pointlessness irritated the others, and my club disbanded after a few months. I can't imagine what I was thinking; perhaps I was looking for the kinds of freewheeling intimacies that a group of girls might have shared in that situation. The name of Duncan's club escapes me. Its function, as far as I can reconstruct it, was limited to perpetual initiation. We were all—Duncan, too—required to pass the tests that Duncan set for us in order to maintain our membership and qualify for the next test.

The initiations were mostly nocturnal events. We lay in bed, fully dressed under our pajamas until the household— usually the McDougals', but sometimes mine—grew quiet. Then, one by one, at intervals of several minutes, we edged barefoot down the stairs like Sioux warriors, the ball of the foot first, then the heel. We regrouped at some prearranged place—the basement of Lehman Hall if it was my house we were coming from, the parking lot behind the infirmary if it was Duncan's. We moved on through the fields to Tom's house, our flashlights pointed down and half-cupped in our palms, shedding only the light we needed to guide our feet. Huddled in the woods beneath his window, we made low hooting noises and waited for his responding echo.

And then Tom was with us. This was the exhilarating moment: our escapes had been successful and we were all together now. We smothered our giggles, whispered, hooked arms. The fall was the best time for these adventures; our transgressions were more thrilling when school was in session. We moved through the cold, wood-smoke–scented air with a magical speed and effortlessness, as though we were still at home in our beds and dreaming. These escapades never lost their power to thrill me, not only in anticipation and retrospect, but actually at the very moments they were taking place. Already, I knew that this was a rare thing.

One of our early destinations was the train station, a few miles from Tom's house. Our dilemma was whether to walk through fields and woods or along the road past the tennis courts and behind the public school. Duncan twisted an ankle by stepping into a gopher hole once—he wore an Ace bandage and limped for weeks, though his mother never noticed—and more than once we got lost in the woods until dawn. But the streetlamps made us visible, and we all lived in dread of the headlights of Chief Royal's cruiser. When a car did come along—the police never did—we plunged into the long grass at the side of the road. I remember seeing headlights splashing up on Duncan's back as he walked ahead of me, his head turning, his glasses flashing white, and his lower lip gleaming. There was no need for alarm: it was only a car packed with Williams students, flicking cigarettes at us and hooting, or an amorous couple in a slow, weaving convertible, ignoring us.

We left pennies on the tracks, waited until the freight train had come and gone, and pried the flattened results off, handing them over to Duncan as tokens of another test passed. Soon we tired of this and moved on to other adventures. We crawled into a coal bin behind Spring Street and came out blackened; it escapes me how I explained that to my mother. On the nights after Williams football games we spread out under the bleachers with our flashlights and collected dozens of church-key openers and pockets full of change, which we duly handed over to Duncan, who divided and redistributed it. We found a pair of fur earmuffs and a half-empty pack of Lucky Strikes, damp but still smokable. We also found a pocket-size aluminum flask containing an ounce or so of Scotch, which Duncan chugged. Once we came upon an obscene snapshot of a nude woman, her head and neck unshown, seated on the tile floor of a dormitory bathroom, her legs spread wide as a pair of male hands intruded into the frame to pry her labia fully open so that the viewer could clearly see the glisten of mucous membrane. That photograph was a prize almost too rich for safekeeping; we debated for a while and decided that I should be the one to take it home and hide it.

We eased into the after-midnight crowds at football rallies. This was a particularly high-risk adventure because of the danger of being spotted by Art Siegenthal, who played with the band, or recognized by our fathers' students. But it was thrilling; the student crowd swayed drunkenly, bawling out spontaneous cheers, their faces savage and ecstatic in the flickering light of the bonfire. We got to hear the bawdy songs and see the off-color skits that were the stuff of legend on the Pine Cobble playground. We watched as Dodson Odetts, a notorious local ne'er-do-well, who bore a strong resemblance to former Senator Joseph McCarthy—the same blue jowls and baleful squint—clambered up on the flatbed truck that served as a stage, and performed his imitation of a woman wriggling into her girdle.

—

It was during one of my parents' parties, just before the move to the white house, that Duncan and Stuart and I sneaked out of the house for the last time. We'd grown bold enough by then simply to walk out the door under cover of the tail end of an extended cocktail hour. I think our destination that night was the system of small caves in the wooded hill above the skating rink behind Spring Street.

When we returned to College Place, well after midnight, we knew immediately that the jig was up. Crouching behind the bushes that lined the parking lot of the fraternity building opposite the library, we saw flashlights moiling up and down in the darkness on Library Hill. Our absence had been noted and the party was out searching for us. James

was out, too: we heard his anxious yips. We also heard giggles from a few of the guests.

Before we could turn and run away, James caught our
scent and flushed us out, barking triumphantly. We were
marched back into the painfully bright light of the house.
The guests were pink-eyed and rumpled at this hour. A few
of my mother's fellow faculty wives were obviously embarrassed for her; they squeezed her hands and murmured sym-
pathetically on their way out the door. I had no way of judging
my father's reaction; he and Lou Behrens of the political science department had stepped into my father's study to conclude a loud, lucid argument about international monetary
policy that had apparently begun earlier in the evening. Meg
McDougal was the only guest to make a comment on our
disappearance and return: she planted her fists on her hips
and demanded to know how it was possible that we had been
able simply to walk out of a house full of adults. But it was
not to Duncan and Stuart and me that she addressed her
complaint: it was to the other guests.

I could see that my mother had caught Meg's implication
that she had somehow been negligent, and I could see that
she was angry. I almost never heard my mother express an
opinion about people we knew, but she made no effort to
hide her feelings about Meg. "*Nymph*omania, *dip*somania, and
puttin' on airs," she used to mutter when she got on that
subject, quoting Truman Capote. She had been particularly

offended when Meg took her aside at the Women's Exchange one day and suggested that I might have an easier time at school if more attention were paid to my clothing and my grooming. "Grooming!" said my mother. "Clothing! Has she taken a look at her own children?"

Duncan and Stuart and Tom were sent home and I was ordered to bed. Andy stood waiting for me at the top of the stairs in his pajamas. His arms were flung open and tears were streaming down his cheeks. "I still love you!" he shouted. The next day my mother told me that there would be no more overnights with Duncan and Stuart. I was ten now, really too old for that kind of thing anyway.

—

And perhaps I was. Around that time Eileen Mannion, who had accused me of deafness when we were both five, marched up to me forthrightly as I sat on the swings after school one day and invited me to spend the afternoon at her house. We had barely spoken in the last five years, but as we walked up the hill together she announced that she had decided we could be friends again. At the outset she made it clear that I had to give up my association with Duncan and Stuart and Tom, and for a while I obeyed. Eventually I began to chafe under her rule, just as I had years earlier when she made me copy her drawings.

Eileen's house stood on a shallow ridge just above the Pine Cobble playing fields, a big Tudor with a long twisting driveway and two fat pillars on either side of the front door. The lawn in back (we had a yard; the Mannions had a lawn) was carefully groomed, and could be described as sweeping. Inside, the rooms were vast and low-ceilinged—not a book in sight—with pale plushy wall-to-wall carpeting and heavy olive green drapes that fell in painterly folds.

Bob and Ramona Mannion were cordial, handsome, and remote. He was a professor of mathematics at Williams, but the Mannions were not intellectuals, not members of my parents' set, though my mother and Ramona were friendly enough when they drew the same shift at the Women's Exchange. Unlike the Barneses and the McDougals, they never invited me to call them by their first names. Eileen, for that matter, would never have dreamed of calling my mother by hers. Even so, her "Mrs. Gordon" carried a charge of presumptuousness that dazzled me and disarmed my mother. As Eileen and I were being driven back to the Mannions' after having dinner at our house, for example, she would lean forward in her seat in the back of the car and invoke the title in her foghorn voice. *"Mrs. Gordon,"* she would say. "Excuse me, *Mrs. Gordon.* I think you asked Emily to clean up her room before supper and I helped her. Do you think we could stop for an ice-cream cone?" And, to my amazement, my mother would.

The Mannions owned two cars and spent their summers on the Cape. But they were also Catholic, and I had picked up the impression that their religious affiliation sat oddly with their languid country-club airs. I remember mumbling self-consciously as grace was said at the dining room table where I sat down with Eileen's family to Saturday lunches of thin roast beef sandwiches, crusts removed. Meals with the Mannions were more decorous than the ones we ate at my house. Eileen kicked me under the table to prompt me to pull the silver monogrammed napkin ring from my loosely furled and slightly grubby linen napkin, then kicked me again to remind me to spread it in my lap.

The Mannions ate all their meals on gold-rimmed china at a mahogany table in the dining room; we ate ours in the kitchen on heavy stoneware plates. We owned linen napkins, but my mother used them only for dinner parties. All four Mannion children—Eileen, her younger brother Paul, and her older siblings Jane and Sandy—were expected to come to the table with freshly washed hands for all three meals, while at our house, dinner was the only meal to which we sat down as a family. At the Mannions' table the food seemed an afterthought, almost a prop, much less important than maintaining good posture and manners and keeping the tablecloth free of stains. At ours the food was complex and delicious and our table manners were mostly ignored, unless my father was feeling irritable. At the Mannions' house the adults drank cocktails before dinner and ice water with it; at ours they drank cocktails before and wine during. At the Mannions', conversation was steady, pleasant, general, and instructive. At our house it was intermittent, occasionally uproarious, and conducted mostly between my parents.

Something about the Mannions brought out the sociologist in me. I found it fascinating to compare them to my own family, and also to the other faculty families I knew. The Mannions were so unlike the McDougals that they seemed to belong to separate branches of the human race. And while the Barneses and the Mannions were both more formal than my parents, their formalities had distinctly different flavors. The Barneses' formality was ironic, aristocratic, southern. The Mannions' formality was suave and worldly, inflected with their Catholicism but kept light by a certain romantic buoyancy.

I remember sitting on the carpet with Eileen one late spring afternoon, scratching the stomach of the Mannions' rheumy-eyed spaniel, and listening to some crooner on the phonograph.

By the sea, by the sea, by the beautiful sea!
You and me, you and me, oh how happy we'll be!

Walking through the room, Ramona Mannion caught the song's rhythm in her knees and executed a series of quick dance steps, a genuflection in the direction of the singer's lilting warble and the cotillions of her youth.

When Eileen was otherwise occupied, I often snooped around Ramona Mannion's skirted dressing table in the master bedroom. I liked to handle her set of tortoiseshell hairbrushes with surprisingly short, soft, apparently useless bristles, and to peer into the cluster of family photographs she displayed on one corner of the table. A number of elderly relatives were represented. Bob was shown as a lanky, smiling young man standing on the beach in a pair of outsize swimming trunks. All four children appeared as infants in their christening robes, and Eileen and Jane had been photographed in their first communion dresses. These smaller pictures were grouped around a silver-framed bridal portrait of Ramona Mannion. The photographer had posed her sitting on a low stool, yards of white satin puddled on the floor around her feet, gazing out into the future with an expression of tranquil, perfectly poised equanimity. Looking at these photographs, I saw that the marriage of Eileen's parents had a shadowy, historical dimension, a chiaroscuro, that my parents' marriage lacked. It was a marriage that progressed in well-defined stages—courtship, engagement, wedding, children, retirement—each time-incursion launched amid a flotilla of photographs, gifts, and letters.

My own parents' wedding had been a hastily arranged civil ceremony held in a judge's chambers on Christmas Day. I've never seen photographs of my mother as a bride, only snapshots taken in the weeks after the wedding when she joined my father at his army base in Kansas. One of them shows my mother, looking young and tired and startlingly pretty, squinting in the harsh afternoon light outside his barracks. My father, in his khaki uniform, stands with an arm slung around her shoulder, his head turned as though someone had just called his name.

What my mother did preserve from their early married days were anecdotes about their life in Cambridge and the set of bright young people they knew there, many of whose names cropped up in the Kennedy administration years later. These friends were full of one-liners that my mother quoted with increasing nostalgia as she grew older. An example: An acquaintance whose girlfriend had left him was found drinking morosely in a bar in the middle of the day. Asked what he was doing, he replied, "Celibating."

My contemplation of the objects on Ramona Mannion's dressing table brought into bold relief something I was just then beginning to understand. What had always seemed solid and inevitable about my parents—their choices, opinions, tastes, and ways—was actually highly provisional. When the Mannions married, they took over the curatorship of an institution, but my parents had deliberately thrown off the burden of family history. They were among the earliest members of a new class, and they were making it up as they went along.

—

Eileen was a tyrant, but I remember her fondly. With her snub nose and curly hair and bumptiousness, she was utterly unlike her smooth parents. She was bossy and intrusive, but I found her bossiness and intrusiveness comforting—at least most of the time. And she was loyal: the very arbitrariness of her judgments kept her suspended a little above the treacherous currents of fashion at school. She was the only friend I'd ever had who stayed my friend on the Pine Cobble playground. If my tormentors approached while we sat on one set of swings, she would take me by the hand and lead me to the set on the other side of the school yard, glaring at them over her shoulder.

Eileen was my first indoor friend; with her there was no wandering. When the children had been excused from the Mannions' table—we had to wait for the parents to give us a nod—she took my hand and pulled me up the stairs and into her room, closing the door behind us. She sat me down on a chair in front of a full-length mirror and made a project of glamorizing me, hanging her sister's pearls around my neck and draping her mother's fur jacket over my shoulders. She brushed my hair back and away from my face—sometimes rather roughly—and pulled it into a tiny tight ponytail. It was too short to stay in place for long, but she tied the collapsing result with a grosgrain ribbon. There! she said, backing away from me and clasping her hands together in satisfaction: You look just like a college girl.

Eileen was always eager to talk, to confide and gossip and compare notes. She gave me a new view of my class at Pine Cobble. I saw it as a hydra-headed monolith, sneering and laughing and shouting insults, but Eileen talked about Jerry Panken and Dixie Wiggins and even some of our teachers as though they were actual people, with vulnerabilities and dimensions I hadn't seen. Oh, *him,* she would say. He just wants the other boys to like him. He's not so bad when you get him alone.

Eileen was a good student and well enough liked, but her life was centered in her family and her summer life on the Cape. More than most children our age, certainly more than me, she was eager for the future. Her parents were doling it out to her in spoonfuls and she was avid to receive it. In just a few more years she would be allowed to go to dances at the club, and the summer after that she could wear off-the-shoulder dresses, and if anyone tried to kiss her she would let him, just to have had the experience. She went on at length about a summer crush she had developed on a friend of her brother Sandy's. She'd met him on the beach. He chased her into the water and splashed her. Could that be taken as a sign that he liked her? And was it all right for her to like *him*—a boy Sandy's age? I said yes on the first count and that I supposed so on the second, though these questions opened up a field of hypotheticals I hadn't yet begun to consider.

She speculated about sex with a blunt specificity that left me speechless. "How would you like having a man put his big thing in you?" she asked me one day as we both sat in front of the mirror applying lipstick. I hardly knew how to answer, but Eileen was interrogating herself more than she was questioning me. "I guess I'd get used to it," she said. "It's part of being married." We were both quiet for a while, each looking into her own eyes in the mirror, unable to stop our minds from following out the implications of that last observation.

I knew almost nothing about Catholicism, only the interesting business about confession. Eileen disappointed me by explaining that of course she would never tell the priest any of the secrets she had confided to me. The sins she disclosed in the confessional were couched in such general terms that the priest could have no idea exactly what bad thing she had done or thought. And really, Eileen pointed out, she couldn't imagine why he would even *want* to know.

What would she tell the priest, I asked her one day, if she hadn't actually committed any sins? There's always something, she answered: an envious thought, a cup left unwashed in the sink. For the sake of argument I pressed her: what if you managed to get through seven days without doing or thinking anything bad at all? That should be possible, I thought, at least theoretically (and wouldn't God wish her to be perfect?). Eileen shrugged: Then I'd make something up.

While it would never have occurred to Eileen to question her religion, her attitude toward it was irreverently instrumental. She accepted the trials and obstacles of her Catholicism the way a hamster accepts the chutes and flywheels in its cage, and she was proud of her skill at negotiating them. When I went to church with the Mannions, she elbowed me in the ribs to prompt me to respond or kneel. "Here comes the money man," she would hiss, pressing a quarter into my palm. She excused me from crossing myself, since I seemed unable to do it correctly.

At that age I was highly susceptible to atmospheres. The air in the church teemed with glittering bits of dust, like the flecks that floated in the bottle of Goldwasser someone had once given my parents as an anniversary present. The hollow percussive echoes of coughs and throat clearings, the rustling nearness of many people, smelling of wool, soap, and cologne, the vault of empty space above my head—all this opened up a longing in my chest. But for what? I had no belief.

I looked up at the statue of the Virgin, wrapped in her blue robe. Her small face was like a hard new bud, her cherry-lipped half smile insipid. What consolation could she offer me? I turned to the stained-glass window depicting Saint

George and the dragon. It was nothing but a cartoon, rendered in garish cartoon colors. I had been trained in my mother's aesthetic and knew what was in good taste and what wasn't. A Quaker meeting hall with worn wooden benches and high, plain, narrow windows was. This church, a glittering jumble of symbolic meanings, wasn't. My mother never spoke disrespectfully of the Mannions and their religion, but now I was old enough to understand her ironic smile when she listened to my stories about attending Mass with Eileen.

The Mannions made it clear—emphatically enough so that I guessed my mother had spoken to them—that I was to stay behind when it was time for the congregation to approach the communion rail. I sat in the abandoned pew, watching as congregants dipped their knees and presented their tongues to receive the host, feeling—not for the last time in my life—like a visiting anthropologist. But no amount of respectful objectivity could banish the sting of exclusion. I wanted to stand up and edge my way into the aisle to join the shuffling herd of souls. I wanted to take the body of Christ on my own tongue and drink the wine that was and wasn't his blood. (Once, as I watched the Mannions take communion, it occurred to me that in the Church, parents become children.) What does the wafer taste like, I asked Eileen. Like nothing at all, she said, and that made me long to taste it even more.

—

Sometime in the spring of our fifth-grade year, I spent the night at the Mannions'. As Eileen and I lay in the dark, she told me that she had an eerie feeling somebody in my family was going to die. This was too much for me, and I began to cry. No, no, said Eileen. Not soon. Just in a while. I was comforted enough by this assurance to go to sleep, but as it turned out, it was someone in Eileen's family who was going to die, and soon. Late that summer, the week before Labor Day, Sandy Mannion, snorkling in the bay at Wellfleet, swam up to the surface for air and was beheaded by the blades of his father's motorboat as his mother and sisters watched from the shore.

My mother told me. The next day Eileen called from the Cape. In the late nineteen fifties, children did not ordinarily place or receive long-distance calls, and as my mother handed over the phone she shot me an uncharacteristically direct look. Eileen said, "I guess you know what happened" with a kind of sheepish shrug in her voice that told me she was deep in shock. Then suddenly she was forgetting herself, talking about some boy at the club in her hot, urgent whisper, stopping in midsentence when she remembered.

It troubles me to recall my reaction to Sandy Mannion's death. I felt no sympathy for Eileen or her family, only a primitive horror and an equally primitive conviction that this news had not come as a surprise. It seemed to me that just as Eileen had expected something bad to happen to our family, so had I been expecting something bad to happen to hers. I suppose I was doing that thing people do—assigning meaning to the meaningless so as to make it meaningful. Even so, I'm a little appalled when I reconstruct my thinking, which was that Eileen and her family had put themselves squarely in the path of calamity. Their belief in God kept them perpetually under His eye. When He was moved by a destructive whim, there they were, all six Mannions lined up at the communion rail, dead center in the bull's-eye. My family, on the other hand, lived in the agnostic shadows outside the range of God's attention. Nothing terrible would happen to us.

You

After the Mannions left for the Cape that summer, I told my mother I wanted to continue going to Mass. She suggested that I comb my hair, put on a skirt and flats, and take a short walk to the Congregational Church on Main Street instead.

I found a place in the back of the church next to a stout man and bellowed out "Old Hundredth" and "A Mighty Fortress" under cover of his bawling baritone. I loved the singing, but the sermons were too reasonable to satisfy me, extended moral quibbles that failed to acknowledge the darker impulses of the human heart and the grosser forms of evil. I knew nothing about such observances then, but if somehow I had been transported from my pew in the First Congregational Church to a Pentecostal tent in Alabama, I wouldn't have hestitated to throw myself on the ground in a twitching, eye-rolling seizure.

My visits to Mass with the Mannions had been my only experience of religion so far, but I was hungry for spiritual intensity. I came into the Congo Church sniffing the air for the odor of sanctity and failed to catch it, though I did detect a whiff of high-minded fellowship. There was nothing in this historic white-clapboard New England church that my mother would consider vulgar: no pie-eyed Virgin, no body-and-blood. But there was nothing very compelling here, either. It was all too stripped-down, too flatly manifest for my taste. Because nothing was hidden, nothing could be revealed.

And there were too many of my classmates' parents in attendance, turning to gawk at me, a child alone in a rear pew. Soon enough, I was taken aside by Mrs. Pearson, one of my mother's fellow pricers at the Women's Exchange (who, as it happened, had casually informed me at age eight that it was better I should know there was no Santa Claus). She led me downstairs to the basement all-purpose room to join a small group of nine- to twelve-year-olds sitting at a folding table. While the congregation sang hymns in the room above us, we spent an hour identifying the religions practiced in various regions of the world, cutting out photographs of Tibetan monks and Russian Orthodox priests from a stack of *National Geographics* and *Life* magazines and pasting them onto sheets of poster board. I lasted only a few weeks in Sunday school, and it wasn't only because there were two smirking Pine Cobblers in the group, nudging one another under the table at the sight of me. It was also because I saw right away that Sunday school was not what I'd come to church for. Everyone, including my mother, had misunderstood my interest in religion. It was initiation I was looking for, not education. In my view, I'd had more than enough of that at school.

———

In Eileen's absence I regressed almost immediately. It took me less than a week to join up with Duncan and Tom once again (Stuart had found other summer friends, and was no longer a steady member of our group). I found them under the skirted pine, and they took me in without remark, as though I had never left them.

One midsummer Friday evening, as the three of us were looping aimlessly around the twilit campus on our bikes, we saw that a dance was getting under way at the Congo Church. The windows of the basement all-purpose room were lit up. Cars were parked along the side and dressed-up teenaged girls were being helped out of them by their fathers. They all wore full skirts in various pastel shades over stiff crinolines of the type I had used to trap my flyaway parakeet. We recognized only one, a public-school girl we had followed and taunted at the skating rink a few years earlier because she had covered her face in pancake makeup to hide her acne.

The girls gathered in a tight circle at the side door of the church, their backs turned to a smaller and looser aggregation of boys who seemed to have materialized out of the darkness. As the chaperone opened the door, Duncan and Tom and I felt the thump of amplified bass in the backs of our knees. At that moment we all formed a simultaneous unspoken intention to crash the dance, or at least to find a vantage point from which to watch it. We knew we were unlikely to be noticed if we sneaked in after the dance had had time to develop, so we swung away on our bikes and rode around the freshman quad for half an hour in the gathering dusk. When we returned it was fully dark. The front doors of the church had been left open, as church doors were in those days. We crept down the side stairs and through a door at the far end of the all-purpose room, secreting ourselves behind a shadowy jumble of upturned tables and room dividers.

The dance floor was a kidney-shaped lagoon of shining linoleum marked off by orange paper lanterns. At its center was a small heap of trucked-in sand anchored by a cardboard palm tree bristling with fronds cut from green construction paper. A pink paper moon hung off center from the ceiling, surrounded by a cluster of aluminum foil stars. The chaperones, church matrons in grass skirts and leis, sat behind a table several yards removed from the dance floor, serving sheet cake and ladling out punch. A man I recognized as an usher from the church stood smoking a cigarette in a far corner of the room, keeping a discreet eye on a section of dance floor blocked from the chaperones' view by the hill of sand and the palm tree. We had arrived in the middle of a self-conscious pause between songs. The girls had retreated to the punch bowl while the boys horsed around and swatted each other among the folding chairs lined up against the opposite wall. For a few minutes it seemed there wouldn't be much to see.

Then the music began and a kind of centrifugal force set the room in motion, drawing and mixing the separated groups together. Some of the boys approached some of the girls and led them away from the neutral territory of the refreshment table and past the barrier of lanterns onto the magical space of the dance floor. Under the eyes of the chaperones, these boys and girls wrapped their arms around one another, some haltingly, some meltingly, and swayed together, shuffling slowly and pointlessly around the desert island in the center of the floor. For the duration of a song, the ordinary rules of interaction were suspended. In their place, the chaperones imposed a kind of martial law. Why, I asked myself, were these ordinarily impermissible embraces allowed? Because there could be no stopping them, was the answer.

I think it was "Earth Angel" they danced to, or "In the Still of the Night," or perhaps it was "Donna." It occurs to me now that before that evening I had never in my life heard music played loud. The tinny consolations of my sister's radio, barely audible behind the closed door of her bedroom, had been no preparation for this. The impact of amplified doo-wop, the steady, insistent beat, the wail of loss and desire, hit me in the stomach and made the breath catch in my throat. My heart lurched, and found a new rhythm.

This, I realized, was it. What was being evoked and enacted in this room was the force that motivated human behavior, a force so powerful that it reached into my own viscera and stirred, mixing feelings that all my life had lain undisturbed in segmented layers into a swirl of confusion and agitated longing. Here was a feeling of the same intensity— though not the same tonal coloration—as the one I'd found in the Catholic church and failed to find at the Congo. Tom stood close to me, staring openmouthed at the dancing couples. Under different circumstances I wouldn't have registered the warm pressure of his shoulder against mine, but now I felt it and wished that he—or someone—would put his arms around me so that we could be like the couples embracing on the dance floor. I wished it so strongly that I interlaced my fingers behind my back to prevent one of my hands from reaching to touch his. But then the pressure of Tom's shoulder was gone. The contact was broken. I saw that Tom and Duncan were leaning together, whispering. The music was too loud for me to catch what they were saying, though I distinctly heard Duncan say the word "boner," and saw Tom shake with laughter.

———

That was the summer we learned boredom. Our clubs were gone, outgrown during the year I'd been off with Eileen. We still wandered, but restlessly, without a sense of urgent purpose. Sometimes we spent afternoons loitering like adolescents in front of the five-and-dime on Spring Street or lolling at the foot of the Haystack Monument, waiting dully for something to happen, our bikes flung on the ground around us, their wheels revolving slowly.

We discovered TV. At Tom's house we helped ourselves to soup bowls full of pretzels and potato chips—his mother had started to go to work during the day—and sat down in the Davises' newly finished basement to watch cartoons and a local children's program called *Freddy Freihofer*. This was an early imitation of *Howdy Doody*, sponsored by a North Adams bakery that has since become a New England–wide corporation with a fleet of delivery trucks. There was a cast of puppet characters—Freddy was a cookie-purveying rabbit—and an audience of children seated on bleachers. It was a rough-and-ready production, rich with bloopers. A golden retriever puppy brought onstage to be fed a bowl of kibble trotted toward the camera instead and sniffed at the lens with his giant quivering nostrils. Led offstage on a leash, he paused briefly to lift a leg and urinate on a little girl's patent leather Mary Jane. Offered a Freihofer cookie, a very small child made a face and announced that he didn't like it. The camera responded by panning away wildly, sweeping past a streaky peanut gallery and coming to a halt with a frozen image of a backstage sawhorse resting on a rumpled dropcloth.

Tom continued to haunt the periodical room in the library and report his findings to us. In a *Time* magazine article he learned about a drug called LSD 25 that caused waking dreams. Researchers in a New York State town not far from us had been performing experiments on themselves, swallowing the drug and recording their reactions. In ordinary states of consciousness, Tom explained, people use only about ten percent of their brains' capacities. Psychedelic drugs might provide access to the other ninety, making it possible for us to make contact with extraplanetary civilizations, or even to see into the future. Mind expansion was one of Tom's obsessions that summer. Another was a story—where he heard it, I don't know—about a gang of anarchists (he knew the meaning of the word, and explained it) who were said to be hiding in the woods above the neighboring town of Pownal. Their leader was a North Adams high school student named Wazniki. According to Tom, the group was preparing to swoop down on the Berkshires to plunder and pillage like a band of latter-day Visigoths. Tom drew a celebratory comic strip showing the anarchist horde, naked except for loincloths, loping through the pines with crossbows strapped to their backs.

Duncan and I were skeptical, but by dint of his persistence Tom persuaded us to ride our bikes to Pownal one morning to find Wazniki. After a few miles it occurred to us that if we planned to hike up into the hills to search for the anarchists, we'd have to leave the bikes by the side of the road, where they might be stolen. So we rode back to Duncan's, ditched the bikes, and set out again on foot, stopping at Sand Springs for sodas. By late morning we hadn't reached the liquor store that marked the Vermont border. Pownal seemed far more distant than it had when I drove through it with my mother on the way to Bennington. The sun rose high in the sky and we grew hot. Duncan asked Tom whether he had a plan for finding Wazniki once we got to Pownal. There were hills all around us, he pointed out. Wazniki and his men might be found anywhere on any of them.

Duncan and I were more attuned to reality than we had

been a year earlier. We were also more sedentary. The summer before we might have pressed on, but we knew better
now. Back at Duncan's we found the house hot and empty.
Hungry after our long walk, we stuffed ourselves with boiled
hot dogs cradled in slices of soft white bread and piled high
with ketchup and relish and the tiny pickled onions used in
Gibson cocktails.

On overcast or rainy days we stayed closer to home than
we once would have, wandering around the campus and
squeezing into college buildings through certain ground-
floor windows we knew to be unlocked. That summer we
developed an enthusiasm for breaking into Chapin Hall, the
auditorium where the Budapest String Quartet played when
they came to the Berkshires, and where the annual John Jay
ski movie was shown. It was fun, and authentically dangerous, to while away a wet summer afternoon edging along the
outside of the balcony railings, forty feet in the air above the
benches and aisles, while the elms lashed in the rain outside.

When that thrill grew stale, we challenged one another to
walk down a hallway that ran the length of Chapin's basement
with the lights off. We called it "the Terror." The artificial
darkness in that hall was purer than any real night could ever
be. In fact it was absolute, said Tom. Duncan scoffed: There is
no absolute darkness anywhere on earth, he insisted, except
possibly deep under the ocean, where the eyeless fish live.

At any rate, the darkness was palpable. I wasn't prepared for the way it seemed to thicken the air and make it hard to breathe, or for the disorientation I suffered. However carefully I lined one foot up in front of the other, I found myself bumbling into the wall on my right. To keep myself straight I moved a few steps to the left and extended my arms, but then I saw a picture in my mind of a razor blade whipping end over end down the hall and amputating my hand at the wrist.

I became conscious of my own tremulous breathing, the rapid thudding of my heart, the amplified squish of my sneakers on the linoleum. That might have been the moment for panic to bloom, but oddly enough I began to feel calmer. I hummed a little tune, very low and soft, so that I felt it in my throat more than I heard it in my ears. The farther down the hall I continued, the more benign and caressing the darkness began to seem. And familiar, too, as though it had been waiting for me all my life. A smile spread itself across my face; I felt as though years ago I'd been told a joke and had only just this moment gotten it. With every step I became bolder, more my own companion, sufficient to myself and fearless, unable for the moment even to remember what fear was. I remembered that walk down the hall in the basement of Chapin Hall as I lay on a delivery table twenty-five years later, doctor and nurses imploring me to push. The same sensation of divine recklessness came to me then, just as I bore down for the last time and felt the liberating squiggle of my daughter's birth.

Just as I found myself wishing that my walk in the darkness could go on even longer—even daring to hope, perhaps, that I might be passing through unseen portals into strange new realms—I bumped into the door at the far end. For a moment I lost my bearings, but when I had turned full circle I saw that the door at the opposite end, dollhouse-size in the long perspective of the corridor, had been etched in radiant apricot-colored light. This was no vision, but electric light from the sconces on the marble walls of the musicians' practice room where Duncan and Tom waited for me. And as I headed back down the hall I saw that all the doors along the way were picked out in faint gray daylight. The darkness had never been absolute, I realized. It had been mixed with light from the moment I set out down the hall.

It was only when my eyes had become accustomed to the darkness that I was able to see the light. Listening to sermons at the Congo Church had given me a feel for homiletic thinking, and walking down the hall I worked to refine this formulation. By the time I reached the end I had it: *Only eyes that have known the darkness can see the light.* I was proud of this pregnant observation, eager to tell my friends about it. Duncan would enjoy having been right and Tom would appreciate the paradox. It was exactly the kind of thing that would impress him.

You

—

I had a few obsessions of my own, and they all bloomed together that summer when I was eleven. They were: my shadow, my smile, and the word "you."

My shadow:

To put it plainly, it was too wide and the sight of it bothered me, especially early in the morning when it was squat as well as fat. But even in the late afternoon, when everyone's shadow grows willowy, I couldn't help noticing that it was thicker than the shadows of most of the people with whom I walked: thicker than my mother's, for example, or my brother's, or Tom's. Only Duncan's shadow, and my father's, continued to be wider than mine. To avoid the recriminating sight of my shadow, I walked with my head twisted to one side and my eyes rolled upward.

My smile:

I had become self-conscious about my teeth. During that summer and for much of the following school year, I tried to solve the problem of my crooked smile by stretching my top lip down so that it covered the uppers and baring my relatively straight bottom teeth instead. I must have made a striking impression, with my chimp's smile and my Egyptian-style walk.

Are You Happy?

There was only one dentist's office in Williamstown when I was growing up. Dr. Andrews occupied it first. In the early years of his practice he used no anesthetic; later he administered novocaine with an instrument that looked like a pastry syringe. His drill was big and slow, with a bass rumble. It fractured enamel the way jackhammers break up asphalt. His practice was primitive, even for those times, limited mostly to tooth filling and tooth pulling, but he was pleasant and children liked him because he invited us to stuff our pockets with penny candy at the end of every visit. When I was nine or ten, Dr. Andrews left Williamstown to join the Army and was replaced by Dr. Johns, who quickly acquired an unfounded reputation as an ogre, probably because his arms and nostrils were hairy and he cut out the candy distribution. He modernized the practice and introduced novelties. I remember being offered a tiny fluted paper cup filled with pink mouthwash—as pretty as an after-dinner cordial—swishing it around in my mouth and leaning over to spew it out into the gently gurgling miniature whirlpool in the bottom of Dr. Johns's newly installed white porcelain spit basin.

My baby teeth had been slow to fall out and tended to co-exist with my permanent teeth as they erupted, leaving me with a double upper row for a few years. By the time I was ten the baby teeth were gone, but they had wreaked havoc with the alignment of my permanent teeth, especially the canines. Dr. Johns was the first in a long line of dentists who have looked in my mouth and deplored the neglect and incompetence of their predecessors. He told my mother I needed braces and referred her to an orthodontist in Pittsfield.

That summer, my father stepped in and took me on a tour of New England dentists, searching for one who would confirm his theory that my teeth would straighten themselves out naturally if given time. His motives were less impure than they might appear. In the service of saving money, he regularly punished himself as well as others. He bought his shirts at Penney's while we lived in Williamstown. In Washington, years later, he bought his suits at Kmart. In the sixties he smoked generic cigarettes. When he traveled he mapped out elaborately indirect itineraries, flying from New York to Washington, D.C., by way of Erie, Pennsylvania, for example, in order to take advantage of anomalies in the fare structures. He himself used the off-brand toothpaste and soap and deodorant he imposed on our household: it wasn't as though he kept a private stock of Ivory and Crest. His cheapness was highly principled, even quixotic. He was willing to spend money in order to save it, ready to incur a net loss in the service of not being had.

I didn't really mind those trips to faraway dental offices. It was pleasant to drive along the two-lane road through sleepy New York State towns, summer air washing in and out of the open windows of the Plymouth. Unlike my mother, who sat tensely upright in the car, clutching the steering wheel with both hands and peering over the dashboard, my father relaxed when he drove. He leaned back in his seat, hummed, rotated his head to work out neck stiffness, draped his right wrist over the wheel and let the other arm dangle out the window, a cigarette lolling between his fingers.

In the car, the war between us was suspended for hours at a time. Alienated though we were from one another, I could tolerate long silences in his company. If someone had asked me to which of my parents I felt closer, I would have said my mother, but in fact I was far more comfortable in my father's presence than in hers. Looking at her, this woman so burdened by her own womanliness, I often wondered how it could be that we were related. Not so with my father: in the car the two of us were like a pair of cats sitting on a windowsill. At any moment, the dominant one might turn to the other and cuff it across the head, but our proximity made a kind of genetic sense.

During those side-by-side hours, I made a study of our similarities. My father was a handsome full-grown man; I was an awkward, overweight preadolescent girl. But there was no doubt that we were constructed on the same lines. Both of us were large boned, short waisted, long legged, and wide hipped, unlike the other members of our family. (An ancient crone, all in black, approached my mother once as our family stood waiting on the platform at the Hillsdale train station. She jabbed a thumb in my direction and ob-

served in a gravelly voice, "She is stout, like her father." Her
point made, she hobbled away.) Our lips were full, our eyebrows heavy and arched, our ears flat and well made. Our
wrists and ankles were narrow, our hands broad, our fingers
long, our thumbs waisted. We were both reflective, easily lost
in thought and reverie. We were both prone to rages. We were
both greedy eaters, always anticipating meals. Our stomachs
had a tendency to rumble in unison.

There were moments in the car with my father when it
seemed to me that it ought to be possible to get along with
him. Of course I knew it wasn't, at least not for long. After a
companionable stretch on the road, for example, we'd stop so
that I could use a gas station bathroom. On my way back to the
car I'd catch sight of his face through the windshield and know
by his expression that he'd been watching me. The moment
I'd seated myself and closed the car door, the berating would
begin. "How come you're the only girl I've ever seen"—
craning his neck, backing rapidly onto the road—"who walks
around"—jerking the car out of its diagonal straddle of two
lanes, flooring the accelerator—"picking her nose in public?"

I don't remember whether or not we found a dentist
willing to let my father off the orthodontic hook, but I never
did get braces. And as it happened, my father was right: in
time, my teeth did straighten themselves out, more or less. I
don't remember the dentists we visited either, except for
the first one in Pittsfield, who gave us a hard sell that infuri-

ated my father. What I do remember fondly about our dental trips were the roadside stands, places where we never would have stopped if my mother had been in the car. My father would catch sight of one of these and pull off the road impulsively, scattering gravel, get out of the car, and return with two hot dogs or two ice-cream cones or two slices of what was then called, in New England, "pizza pie." Sometimes we stopped at Howard Johnson's and sat at the counter. My father ordered a club sandwich with potato chips and a cup of coffee. I ordered a clam roll and a peppermint hot fudge sundae.

The word "you":

For some reason, "you" took up residence in my mind that summer and could not be evicted. "You," I subvocalized as I tied my sneakers in the morning. "You, you, you," I muttered as I backed my bike out of the garage. Whenever anyone spoke the word, I heard it amplified and isolated from the words that surrounded it. When I spoke it I felt a small self-conscious thrill, as though I had inserted a coded secret into my ordinary speech.

It would be nice to think that the discovery of "you" was evidence that I'd recognized the reality of other people, and I suppose it was, if only incidentally. But "you" did not mean *them.* It meant them meaning *me,* them recognizing my reality—whether they wanted to or not. And when I addressed those others, using the word "you," I laid claim to recognizing theirs. I could say "you" to anyone. The language itself, locking its users into reciprocity, gave me permission.

I entertained fantasies about belonging to a vaguely imagined society of beings who lived in a widemouthed cave with a sandy floor, very much like a diorama of an early Homo sapiens habitation I once saw at the American Museum of Natural History in New York. These communards—I think I must have picked up the notion of collectivism from my father's dinner party talk—wore forest-green leather jerkins and peaked caps, like extras in a Robin Hood movie. They were male and female, of indeterminate age, though young, and their faces were blank ovals. Their interchangeability was part of their appeal; in this ideal society, no face but my own was necessary. My imagination had never provided these people with occupations; mostly they squatted over small fires or scrawled unreadable messages in the sand with sticks. Their function was to recognize me. They were the you-sayers. "You!" they cried out at the sight of me, rising as a body to their feet to approach and surround and draw me into their circle, "You! You! You!"

—

The summer progressed. Tom and I began to wander off together, leaving Duncan in front of the TV in the Sommerses' basement. We followed a path through the dense woods behind Tom's house that led us past a swimming pool in back of the brown-shingled apartment building where James Finney Baxter's secretary lived. (Gooseberries grew near there, tiny translucent rubbery-skinned beach balls, juicy but disappointingly bland and only faintly sweet, like figs.) The path wove on through a dark pine woods and around a recently built and still uninhabited split-level house, broken into periodically by teenaged boys who left a trail of crumpled beer cans behind them. I stepped on a used condom on the path near that house once. Tom scooped it up with a stick and flung it into the trees.

We came out of the woods into a sloping meadow. At its base was a barn, our unacknowledged destination. As we lay on our backs on a stack of baled hay, swallows darting back and forth in the rafters above us, I told Tom that I had learned to use telepathy to talk to animals. He swallowed this whopper whole, never once asked me to demonstrate the occult skill I claimed to have discovered in myself, not even when a feral cat arched its back and spat at us.

Why this lie? Because it was irresistible—Tom was so credulous, so eager to be amazed—and because it elicited the ripest, most radiant "you's" that had ever been addressed to me. When did YOU first realize that YOU could talk to animals? he asked me, sitting bolt upright and staring down at me with his guileless blue eyes. Do YOU find it easier to talk to some kinds of animals than others?

My lie was an inspired first move in what I had begun to realize was a flirtation. It riveted Tom, silenced his stream of talk about warrior trials among the Sioux and herbal cures used by Amazonian tribes and fixed his attention on me. It was this lie that elicited a look I couldn't remember ever having seen in anyone's eyes before, a slow, wondering look of fascinated reappraisal that made me want to simper and pirouette like a four-year-old.

On one of our walks, after some hemming and hawing and self-conscious snorts of laughter, Tom told me that recently he realized who it was I reminded him of. It was Ann Sothern on *The Ann Sothern Show*. I was stunned by this confession; it seemed incredible that Tom could identify me with this short, busty blond with her hooded eyes and coyly pursed lips and her habit of standing on tiptoe and thrusting her bosom into the camera space between herself and whatever befuddled male she was addressing in her capacity as executive secretary or hotel manager—I don't remember which.

Ann Sothern? It was something about her, Tom explained. He couldn't put his finger on exactly what. But I knew, though I couldn't have articulated it then. It was the counterfeit knowingness, the fraudulent aura of mystery I had draped over myself when I told my ridiculous lie about talking to animals. That made me female to Tom and put me in the company of Ann Sothern. No doubt he realized that she and I were located very far apart from one another on the continuum of femininity. But the category itself was a new discovery for him, so perhaps the matter of *degree* of femininity was not particularly important. It's also possible that Tom's imaginative powers were so highly developed that he was able to borrow some of Ann Sothern's hyperfeminine attributes and graft them onto me, merging us into a chimera, a blend of unthreatening friend and exotic siren.

August came; in the evenings the crickets on Library Hill were singing "Six weeks till frost." Tom and I continued our walks and our sessions of lying on our backs in the hay barn. Some kind of culmination was in the air. An avowal? A kiss? Both? I tried to imagine my arms around Tom, his around me. It was a pleasant enough sensation, if a little indistinct. I seemed to have lost access to the longings I felt when he and I stood shoulder to shoulder in the all-purpose room of the Congo Church, watching couples dance to "Donna."

Here is what happened. It still mortifies me. As we lay on our pallet of hay in the barn one afternoon, staring up at the sunny chinks that riddled the roof, Tom turned to me and asked, in a strangled whisper, if I could please stand up. I did. He knelt behind me and asked me to pull down my pants and underpants. I remember the sensation of air around my upper thighs. Could you . . . he asked, . . . could you bend your knees just a little? I moved into a semi-squat. No, said Tom. Not that much. There. Yes.

I had no idea what Tom's intention was, but soon enough it became evident. Kneeling behind me on the straw, he explored the contours of my buttocks, palpating them with his gifted hands. He touched them gently, tentatively at first. Then, more vigorously, he kneaded them. "If there is a God," he declared, his voice hoarse and deeper than the one I was used to hearing, "he made you beautiful!"

———

My mother sewed many of her own clothes and some of mine and my sister's as well. She chose pastels for Katy and darker, earthier colors for me. Every year just before school started, she ran me up two A-line jumpers with patch pockets on her Singer. They were made of narrow-wale corduroy in two of four colors: brick red, olive green, navy blue, and mustard. I wore them with blue or white oxford-cloth shirts, kneesocks, and oxblood oxfords. For years, this had been my school costume.

That summer, with a few weeks of vacation remaining, my mother took a long look at me at the breakfast table one morning. She called me up to her third-floor sewing room and measured my chest, waist, and hips, jotting down the dimensions in faint pencil in a small notebook, from which I averted my eyes.

We drove to the fabric store in Bennington. My mother picked out the pattern, a new one this year. It was a dress, not a jumper, with an Empire waist and long sleeves. For the first time, I was allowed some say in the choice of fabric. While she browsed in the buttons and notions, I walked up and down the aisles. Something about a heavy plum-colored material with a dull sheen stopped me. I ran a finger down the bolt; I liked its silky feel, its barely perceptible bumpiness. I called my mother over. "No," she said. "That's upholstery fabric. This whole wall is upholstery. Try over here."

The sailcloth I drew to her attention had unbecoming vertical stripes. The beige linen was not my color. To demonstrate, she took me to a mirror and held it under my chin. The effect was lost on me; I saw nothing, only my face, no worse and no better than usual. My mother excused herself and went out to smoke a cigarette in the Plymouth. I walked among the bolts, paralyzed by indecision and self-doubt. Colors, textures, patterns, and all the permutations that combining them generated: How could I know what was appropriate? Or what I wanted? There was a whole system of unwritten rules here; I'd just have to guess. Then my mother was at my side, holding a swatch of fabric. "What about this?" she asked. "It's just a remnant. There may not be enough yardage."

It was a heavy black cotton, printed with a scatter of pink blossoms and green leaves—like a spring evening. My mother draped it over my shoulders and led me back to the mirror. The effect was subtle but transformative. The reversal of light and dark in the fabric made my eyes shine and my skin glow. It made me pretty. Standing a little behind me in the mirror, my mother looked serious and pleased. We picked out some matching lime green rickrack for the neckline of the dress and three silver buttons for the bodice.

My mother knelt on the floor in her sewing room, pinning pieces of the pattern to the material, then cutting along the dotted lines with her special sewing scissors, a formidable implement that crunched through fabric in long swaths. I stood over her, helpless in my ignorance and clumsiness, but proprietary about the progress she was making on my dress, about which I'd been thinking day and night since we brought the fabric back from Bennington.

My mother made an effort to teach me how to sew, but I was easily confused by concepts like "front" and "back." Eventually, to keep me out of her hair while she worked on the dress, she gave me a skirt to hem. That I could do, but so slowly and ham-handedly that eventually she yanked it out of my hands and finished it herself. I was useful for threading needles—"I need your young eyes, Em," she would say— but beyond that I was no help as a seamstress's assistant.

I never learned to sew. Still, my mother passed on to me

a little of the vocabulary and lore of sewing and clothes design. An A-line dress "hides a multitude." A straight skirt
with a back zipper is a "trying line." When my mother
scolded me for using "a lazy woman's thread"—to save myself the trouble of rethreading the needle, I'd cut too long a
piece—I heard the voices of my grandmother and my York-
shire great-grandmother in the phrase.

I eased my arms—"Carefully, carefully," said my mother—
through the sleeves of the basted-together dress. She zipped
up the back, then hovered over me making adjustments at
the waist and the neckline, her eyes darting, her mouth bristling with pins. A Kent was left smoldering in her oversize
ashtray. She spoke very little, occasionally mumbled to herself under her breath. I was hardly present to her, except
as a mass to be accommodated. Still, there was something
deeply reassuring to me about being there with my mother
in her sewing room. While she worked on this project she
was too absorbed to be unhappy. There was no toneless
humming, no harsh sighing.

When the dress was finished and hemmed, I put it on and
my mother and I both went downstairs and stood before the
full-length mirror on the closet door in her bedroom. My
mother stood behind me and a little to one side, as if presenting me to my reflection, or my reflection to me. The
dress did as much for me as a dress could do, which wasn't
as much as I had hoped. But the colors were becoming and

the neckline was flattering and the line of the bodice anticipated, if only faintly, the development of my bust and waist.

I remember the black-flowered-dress project as a brief
rapprochement between my mother and me, before her un-
happiness had taken her too far away to be reached. It was
not a return to our old love, but it was a gesture of care, an
acknowledgment of the imminent arrival of a new stage in
my development, a casual offer of inclusion in the company
of women.

Trenton Is the
Capital of New Jersey

When the Mannions returned from the Cape after Labor Day, everyone saw that Sandy's death had aged his mother and made her beautiful. People gazed at her admiringly and murmured to one another as she walked down Spring Street or along the aisles of the A&P, lowering their eyes instinctively when she came closer. The faculty wives made room for her at the Women's Exchange pricing table and let do her work unmolested by gestures of sympathy. My own mother spoke of Ramona Mannion with emotion; all her life she fiercely admired women who kept up appearances in the face of grief.

As for Eileen, I took one look at her and saw that she was

lost to me. Over the summer the estrogens had been doing their work, smoothing her features and bringing them into a closed, completed harmony. Like a bud forced into early bloom, she had developed a waist and the beginnings of breasts. Suddenly she was a pretty young girl, and I was still a child.

After a month or so I called Eileen at my mother's prompting and invited her to spend the night at our house. Her mother declined for her and invited me to come to theirs instead, but only for dinner. I dreaded that visit, but when I sat down at the Mannions' table I saw that I would be able to get through the evening: this was my first intimation of how much stretch is inherent in the idea of "bearable." A conscious decision had apparently been made to maintain the usual routines and customs; we lined up to wash our hands in the little half bathroom across the hall, just as we always had. We dried them on the bath towel, not the hand towels, just as we'd always been told to do. We lowered our heads as Eileen's father said grace, which he did in his usual perfunctory way. The atmosphere was less grim than I had expected; at one point both parents laughed at something that Eileen's younger brother blurted out. Everything was very much the same, only a little muted.

But Eileen was utterly changed. Not only was she pretty and tall; she was suddenly quiet, self-contained, and dutiful. At the end of dinner she stood up and began clearing the table.

Startled, I got to my feet and carried my plate away, stopping
to pick up Paul's silverware and water glass. As Eileen passed
her mother on the way to the kitchen, Ramona Mannion
looked up. Her face fell out of its social composure and relaxed into lines of natural grief and intimate gratitude. She
smiled at her daughter, her eyes shining with tears.

——

My sixth-grade teachers were the talented Mr. Yaple (Biology), the Anglophilic Miss Bond (English), Mrs. Pierce
(Math), M. Rustin (French), and Mr. O'Malley, a snide brute
in his early forties with foul breath and a missing thumb joint
(Geography and Homeroom).

Mr. O'Malley had a habit of winging pieces of chalk at
woolgatherers. One of these missiles caught me under the
eye and left a mark; he launched it just as I turned from gazing out the window. My mother drew her breath in sharply
when she saw the small bruise on my face, though she said
nothing about it. Nobody had any notions about abuse in
those days, and in spite of her liberal pedagogical beliefs, it
would never have occurred to her to protest any punishment
a teacher gave me.

One day, as he patrolled the aisles of the classroom, Mr.
O'Malley looked down and saw that instead of composing
the assigned theme, I'd been occupying myself by writing

"relax" over and over in my loose-leaf notebook, enclosing each word in an oval shaded with fine crosshatchings. (I was imitating my sister, who doodled eloquently in the margins of the notebooks she brought home from boarding school.) He ripped the page out and held it aloft. "How many of you think that what Emily Gordon needs to do is to . . ." He held the paper an inch from his nose and squinted, as if puzzling out an illegible word. ". . . *relax*? Let's see a show of hands." No hands were raised.

"No," he went on. "On the contrary. The last thing in the world that Emily Gordon needs to do is to *relax*. She *relaxes* far too much already. What she needs to do is to *apply* herself, wouldn't you say?" There was a low murmur of assent and my heart lifted because I could hear the reluctance in it. Mr. O'Malley crushed the paper into a ball in his fist and dropped it on my desk, then squatted on his haunches and whispered "twenty-five laps" in my ear. I'd been bracing for that: his halitosis was worse than any punishment. I held my breath until he'd gotten up and moved away—made a furtive but self-dramatizing show of it, hunching my shoulders and bugging my eyes, to get what sympathy I could from my classmates. The very popular Dixie Wiggins shot me a friendly look—or a look that might reasonably be interpreted as friendly. I was quick to appreciate the uses of Mr. O'Malley's cruelty. On any day when he gave me a hard time in the classroom, I could expect my tormentors to give me a pass on the playground.

———

Another obscure social law began to operate in the early months of sixth grade. Instead of pushing its peripheral members further away from its center, the group had begun to draw them in. As if some invisible gear had been thrown into reverse, the wheel of fortune seemed to have halted over the summer, and now it was turning in the opposite direction. The force at work here was Eros. Sex had been a joke, but now it was active in our lives, and this was the year the kissing game parties that regulated and institutionalized it began.

Full attendance was expected at these events; everyone had a part in the sexual drama, even if the role called only for repeated rejections. On the one occasion when I drew the short stick, the boy with whom I was paired groaned loudly and smote his forehead, and all the other boys laughed, but by now I had seen enough to understand that this reaction was a convention. Nearly all the girls evoked these protests; only two or three of the most precociously nubile were received in cowed silence. I found the groaning and forehead smiting almost reassuring; it could be taken as evidence that I had been folded into the group.

Three or four of these parties were held over the course
of the fall semester, one disguised as a birthday celebration.
A few were improvised on weekends and held in the basement of Lehman Hall, but they were not successful. Careful
organization and planning were required to impose a ran-
domizing game structure on these gatherings and facilitation
was needed to procure the consent of the participants; otherwise nobody could get up the nerve to do the actual kissing. Instead, we reverted to our natural social patterns: the
girls huddled together and the boys distracted themselves
with horseplay. A few misfits of both genders—I was one of
them—wandered or sat alone.

Jerry Panken was our leader and host. The official kissing
parties were held at his house, a newly built Colonial behind
a popular steakhouse and hotel on Cold Spring Road, owned
by his father. I had never set foot inside the 1896 House, and
neither had my parents. To me it had always been associated
with Republicans and golf and the House of Walsh, all those
influences I had grown up considering noxious. (Confusingly,
the Pankens were Jewish.) Before the first party began, Jerry
gave us a tour of the restaurant. We walked through the
wood-paneled lounge, where the bartender sat behind the
bar wiping glasses with a linen napkin. A barmaid stood on a
stool polishing a great mirror that doubled the count of the
bottles lined up behind the bar and reflected a lone patron
sitting at a table in a patch of sun by a window—it must have

been four o'clock in the afternoon—reading the *Berkshire Eagle* and drinking something amber from a short glass. I made up my mind right then to come back when I was of age and sit at that bar and order drinks, and I did.

Jerry Panken was only twelve, and tiny for his age, but he had a prematurely jaded look. His heavy eyes and rakishly off-kilter smile made him look like a French cabaret singer—at least, from the neck up. In fifth grade he'd been fairly far back in the pack, but in sixth we all became aware of his late-blooming aptitude for style. Jerry Panken was a prophet of hipness. With his disproportionately long pipe-stem legs, he wore tight jeans well. And they were soft and faded, not the stiff boxy dungarees our mothers bought at Penney's. Many of the boys, and a few girls, imitated his habit of wearing oversize flannel shirts untucked, the sleeves rolled up past the elbow and the top three buttons left open, over waffle-patterned long johns. And nearly everyone tried to copy the way he wore his ski hat, not pulled down over his ears like a baby but perched loosely on the very top of his head so that only his thick curls held it in place.

Jerry's parents were rarely in the house during the day, so we had the use of the big walk-in closet off the master bedroom. When it came my turn to walk into the darkness, it was with Dennis Minot, a big pudgy boy with a crew cut and a rabbity overbite, the only child of an overprotective mother. He lived in one of the small pastel houses below

Southworth Street, near Mrs. Imhoff's nursery school. We had ridden the school bus together in third grade and teased and punched each other companionably, but in fifth grade he'd grown three inches and gained thirty pounds. For that he was awarded a position among my tormentors on the jungle gym.

Once the door to the closet was closed behind us, we were required to kiss nonstop for three minutes, Jerry Panken's father's dress shirts rustling at ear level, while the crowd outside in the bedroom hooted encouragement and insults and Jerry Panken timed us. We did kiss briefly. How cool and soft his lips felt, how confiding and friendly! It was as though he had been waiting for just such a private moment to apologize for the year he'd spent tormenting me. But soon the kissing began to seem pointless and exhausting, so we whispered jokes, holding each other loosely and suppressing our giggles. I never felt a moment's sexual arousal or romantic transport while I huddled in that closet with Dennis. What I felt was happiness.

—

I've often described myself as a dreamy child, so I find it disconcerting to acknowledge how few actual fantasies I can actually recall. The cave-dwelling you-sayers was one, but it was so thinly imagined and psychologically transparent that it hardly seems to count. And there was another I had at age twelve that involved being married to an African diplomat, a very dark and round man in a blue and gold robe with a face as benign and indistinct as the man in the moon's. But this was a transitional fantasy that carried a heavy freight of disguised eroticism; it belonged to adolescence more than to childhood.

I never entertained the Walter Mittyish waking dreams that everyone associates with the years of latency, never found consolation by imagining myself as a ballerina or a princess. These kinds of fantasies have always seemed a little crass to me, like praying to God for money or for victory in an election. But perhaps the real problem was simply that I knew all too well how I'd look in a tutu or a tiara.

My specialty was never self-idealizing fantasy; instead it was the cultivation of certain odd states of reception. By the time I reached sixth grade I had been working at this ability for years, and had become something of an adept. Like a dog sniffing its way through a meadow, I'd found places all over Williamstown where I was likely to catch the scent of whatever it was I was after.

There was, for example, a certain prospect, an amphitheater of flat stubbled fields that opened up to me just as I came around a bend in the tire track road that led to the pond where we skated in winter. There was nothing picturesque about this view, just an idiosyncratic spatial magic, something I was sure I could never convey to any other person. It was no more communicable in words than a color would be, or a single musical note.

The very best spot for reception was in the basement of the Williams College student union building. I made my way down there after school whenever I could during the fall of my sixth-grade year, through the student lounge and past the pool tables to a small viewing room where films like *Pather Panchali* and *Bad Day at Black Rock* were shown to faculty family audiences on Friday nights. My fascination with this room had nothing to do with any cinematic interest. What I found so compelling was an area of damaged acoustic tile on the ceiling, eight or ten squares yellowed by water staining and etched with fissures and faint tracings that suggested a map of the tributaries of the Euphrates. There were panels of fluorescent lights on either side of this manifestation, but I knew better than to turn them on. The dim gray light that filtered through the venetian blinds was enough for young eyes to see by; more would have blasted away the effect I was looking for. I sat down in a chair directly under the damaged tiles and let my arms flop at my sides and my head loll back. I must have made a strange sight to students passing by in the hall outside. After a few minutes of contemplation I could depend on receiving a concentrated thrill, a sensation of direct apprehension of historical time, as though the tiles had been soaking in some distilled essence of all the centuries.

These states were oddly emotionless. There was no melancholy or joy or anger in them. I believed that they were made of the world, not of my feelings, and I would have insisted on this point if anyone had challenged it. My reaction was a moodless registration—a key turning and a tumbler falling.

In another child, this odd game I played with myself might have grown into an academic engagement with the study of history. Still another, operating at a higher level of abstraction, might have made an empirical survey of ceiling tiles in other rooms and other buildings. But the historical way was not my way, and the scientific way was even less so. It's hard to retrieve the odd thought processes of childhood, but I think I had an idea that learning was inimical to my states of reception, that knowing about the world might block the direct access to its essences that I felt I had achieved. I believed that the whole enterprise depended on an acceptance of the world exactly as it was laid out. There could be no investigation, no categorization, no redistribution, no attempt to view this phenomenon under the aspect of anything but itself. I was primitive enough to believe that any tampering with the mysteries in this room would be punished by a swift and brutal revocation of all the magic in the world—something like the blighting winter visited on the earth by Demeter when her daughter was exiled to Hades.

The feelings I got from looking up at the ceiling tiles had to do with the past, but I also understood them as harbingers of the future. I believed that if I waited long enough, what-ever it was that I had glimpsed briefly in the viewing room would return, and that this time it would be disclosed to me in all its fullness.

—

At school I was floundering, in English now as well as in my other subjects. Unlike my earlier teachers, Miss Bond made no allowance for my aptitude or for my mother's feelings; the themes I composed for her were returned to me marked with Cs and Ds, mechanical errors heavily underscored in red ink.

In French class I started strong; my crush on M. Rustin gave me an incentive to memorize vocabulary. He was a Williams senior, short and swarthy, Napoleonic-looking, with a big head and an imperious strut. One Saturday afternoon he invited a group of us to his dorm room. We admired his Toulouse-Lautrec posters and listened to his Edith Piaf records, balanc-ing demitasses half-filled with hot chocolate on our knees. In December M. Rustin chose three girls from the class—he was something of an impresario on campus, organizing festivals and directing plays—to sing French Christmas carols at an evening service at the Williams chapel. Amazingly, I was one of them. We walked down the aisle wearing long white robes designed by M. Rustin and sewn by our mothers, and wreaths of pine needles in our hair. Each of us carried a thick white candle resting in a nest of holly. M. Rustin kissed us on our foreheads as we emerged from the vestry room, and whispered in my ear that my voice was the loveliest of all. An extremely happy moment, and a happy memory to keep, but even so I did badly in French. I could never seem to get the knack of conjugating verbs.

In Geography, Mr. O'Malley declared that if I learned nothing else that semester, he would see to it that I would never forget that Trenton is the capital of New Jersey. For a week I stood on a low stool in the empty classroom every afternoon after school and wrote out "Trenton is the capital of New Jersey" fifty times on the blackboard. After a few days I discovered that it was much quicker and easier on the arm to make vertical columns of each word, starting with

TRENTON

TRENTON

TRENTON, etc.

and going on to write fifty iterations of

IS

IS

IS

and so on with "the" and "capital" and "of" and "New" and "Jersey." Once I hit upon this method, I found I no longer minded writing out sentences on the blackboard. By automating the project, I could tell myself that I was constructing a kind of art object or concrete poem. At the same time, I was sabotaging the purpose of the exercise by breaking up the sense of the sentence—observing the letter of Mr. O'Malley's punishment but not the spirit. That gave me a certain subversive satisfaction.

In Math, the class had moved on to algebra and I was irretrievably lost. I sat with Mrs. Pierce at her desk in the empty classroom two afternoons a week, working backward through textbooks until she found my level of competence, which must have been first or second grade. Then we ground slowly forward, under cover of reviewing what I'd forgotten. In truth, I was learning this material for the first time, but having learned it now, I forgot it almost immediately. Mrs. Pierce would quiz me on material I'd seemed sure of two days before, and it would be gone.

Occasionally, I'd look up from the problem with which I was struggling and catch her staring at me with gentle incredulity in her tired eyes. How exhausted she looked! She was a rangy farm wife from nearby Stephentown, New York, kind, laconic, and a little grim, a mother of five who milked the cows every morning and played the violin in a local chamber-music ensemble. By Thanksgiving she had given up on me, and I was left to practice my doodling in my notebook in the back of the classroom while the other students solved equations at the blackboard.

One day as I sat twisting and twirling on the swings at recess, Mrs. Pierce came striding across the playground toward me with a look of purpose. She was carrying a book, a collection of poems, one of those anthologies of nineteenth-century chestnuts that school libraries were full of in those days. She stood watching me, her arms crossed over her chest, while I read the poem she had bookmarked. I can't recall the author or even the title. It was an extended exhortation, floridly written, urging me to lift my eyes and look past the tribulations of the moment toward a glorious future that awaited me just beyond the horizon.

I realized in later years that Mrs. Pierce was a genuine well-wisher, one of several I knew in my childhood. But as she stood over me there on the Pine Cobble playground I was so panicked and irritated that I could hardly take in the poem's meaning. She seemed to have no idea that our interaction might draw attention. Anything out of the ordinary could bring my tormentors—still active, though recently they'd been leaving me alone during recess—over to investigate. Was she going to leave the book with me? The moment she was gone, Stephen Flagg would snatch it away and read the poem aloud in a fluting voice, with accompanying hand gestures. But apparently she was determined to stand there stubbornly in her car coat and earmuffs, waiting for me to finish. When I handed the book back to her, she raised her eyebrows significantly and walked away. (I remember the backs of her calves, meaty as drumsticks and fish-belly-white under her seamed stockings.) Later I asked myself: How did she know? I had thought my mother and I were the only ones who understood that I was marked for a special destiny.

—

Academically, I continued to fail, but by the end of the semester my social fortunes had begun to turn. My first piece of luck was that Caroline Bahnson came to work at Pine Cobble as girls' sports coach. Right away, she instituted some reforms that the faculty-wife faction at Pine Cobble had been urging for years. She dropped the practice of allowing captains to "choose up" teams thus subjecting the unathletic and unpopular to daily humiliations, and she cut back on the lap running; when Mr. O'Malley ordered twenty-five, she allowed me to run ten and walk fifteen. Instead of jumping jacks and push-ups, she taught us limbering-up exercises adapted from modern dance and short sets of easy calisthenics.

The girls hectored and adored her, mobbed her as she sat cross-legged on the sidelines, begged for the privilege of combing out and braiding her horse's tail of strawberry-blond hair. I hung back a little, understanding that my early intimacy with the Bahnsons created a certain conflict of interest. Some instinct told me to conceal that connection from the other girls. Perhaps this was my first socially shrewd act, and Caroline seemed to understand. But I was the one she kept at her side when we all walked across the frozen fields to the pond to skate, the one she chose to help her gather up the sticks and balls and kneepads after field hockey practice.

In November I took up skiing and sprained my ankle— my second piece of luck. Skiing had been an enthusiasm at Pine Cobble since third grade, but in sixth grade it turned cultic. Equipment was an obsession, and Jerry Panken was the arbiter of correctness. Head skis were the only right kind, and a certain brand of square-toed ski boot. There was an impenetrable mystique concerning the various kinds and colors of waxes and their uses in different weather and snow conditions. Jerry set the pace by wearing heavy gray knee-high socks emblazoned with red and black snowflakes and waist-length parkas stuffed with goose down and water-proof pants that zipped up the sides, all available at the House of Walsh. He wore tinted goggles on the slopes, shov-ing them up onto his forehead when he parked his skis on the rack outside the hot, dark lodge and clomped in to the counter to order a hamburger.

I owned none of these things. My skis came from the Sears cataolog. I wore mittens, not fur-lined leather gloves, and high-waisted dungarees that soaked through at the first contact with snow and rubber galoshes over several pairs of heavy socks and a knee-length loden coat with wooden toggles.

Even so, I begged my mother to take me to Dutch Hill every weekend. Oddly enough, skiing made me happy, or at least riding the T-bar did. I was afraid of it at first, but after I learned how to catch the bar one-handed as it came swinging up behind me and how not to let the initial jerk unseat me, I came to love it so much that I reimagined it as I lay in bed at night. My guilt at the effortless pleasure of the ride was assuaged by the easy task of keeping my skis aligned in the rippling ruts cut by the skis of all the riders ahead of me, a job that grew trickier when tall pines sprang up on either side and the air turned sharply colder and the grade grew so steep that I had to draw my knees up to my chest. Then the ground leveled and I emerged into an open stretch of white dazzle, feeling the winter sun pour down on my shoulders and back—like hot fudge, I always thought, on vanilla ice cream. At the summit I straightened my legs and let the T-bar leap away from me. It jounced up in two bounds to the top of the cable tower, where it spun like a propeller on a beanie and was sent sailing down the mountain again.

The problem facing me now was how to get to the bottom of the slope without injury or loss of dignity so I could take another ride on the lift. I never really learned to ski, never progressed beyond a timorous snowplow. My feet grew numb with cold and my inadequately supported ankles ached. I was terrified of falling or colliding with a tree, afraid of the shouts of my schoolmates—the few who happened to be slumming it on the beginner's slope that day— as they whipped past me, bent at the waist, their elbows tucked into their sides, their narrow hips swiveling.

I learned to slow my progress by transecting the slope in shallow diagonals, grinding to a stop at the tree line and turning myself around by stamping a fan in the snow. From this vantage point I could see as far as my eyes would allow, past the sheltering ring of mountains that surrounded me every day—there was Mount Greylock, with its orienting hump—to the interwoven ranges beyond them, fading from purple to violet to gray and growing paler still until I could no longer distinguish the mountains from the sky.

One afternoon as I was taking one of my cautious passes across and down the slope, I felt a rush of air on my cheek and turned to see that an elderly skier was barreling down the hill straight toward me, his face contorted with rage. We avoided a direct collision, but the tips of his skis ran under mine and we fell into a sprawling, sliding tangle. When we came to rest twenty yards or so down the hill, the old man picked himself up, cursed me, brushed the snow off his pants, and continued down the mountain at a chastened speed.

One of my skis had come loose and gone shooting into the woods. My other leg was twisted and pinned under me at an unnatural angle, and tears were running down the slopes of my cheeks, filling my ears and dampening the brim of my hat. After a few moments I realized that I was more stung by the old man's behavior than I was hurt, but then my ankle began to throb. One skier after another whizzed past and I wondered if I would be left on the mountain to freeze. I imagined the sun setting over the mountains, chilly and pink, the pines turning inky, the first stars blinking.

Just as I was considering the idea of trying to get onto my feet, the ski patrol arrived. I was loaded onto a toboggan, covered in blankets, secured with straps, and escorted down the mountain to the first-aid lodge, where one of the members of the ski patrol palpated my ankle tenderly and another brought me a small glass of brandy and a third sat on the edge of my cot and did his best to make me laugh. (He had taken me to be a boy at first, but when I took off my hat he apologized gallantly.) By the time my mother arrived I was reluctant to leave, but then there was the pleasure of being carried out on a stretcher under a starry sky to the parking lot and being lifted into the back of the Plymouth. After that, there was still more attention at Dr. Steinglass's office and a trip to the hospital in North Adams for my first X-ray. I was disappointed to learn that my ankle was not broken, only badly sprained, but the doctor wrapped it in a bandage thick enough to be taken for a cast from a distance.

For six weeks I walked on crutches. At Pine Cobble there

was enormous prestige in skiing injuries—for all his equipment, Jerry Panken had never had one—and crutches were objects of envy. Oddly enough, I was more graceful on them than I had ever been on my feet. After a week I was negotiating the narrow halls and stairways confidently, stowing the crutches in a corner of the classroom and hopping to my desk on one foot, just as I had seen others do. Toward the end I took to using only one crutch, swinging through the halls with abandon and rounding corners recklessly. My teachers were solicitous and my tormentors let me pass in silence. Caroline Bahnson carried a wooden stool out to hockey practice in the afternoons and let me sit out the games next to her.

———

By the time we came back from Christmas vacation, my stock had risen considerably. Mr. O'Malley's persecution and my special relationship with Caroline Bahnson and my crutches had brought me to the edge of acceptibility. The arrival of Marjorie Martinelle was my third piece of social luck, and it put me over the top.

For every social role that is vacated, a new occupant soon appears, and Marjorie Martinelle was my replacement as class pariah. She was a transfer student from the public school, the daughter of a prosperous dairy farmer, a matronly girl who walked ploddingly, as though she were carrying milk jugs in both hands. She had a downright way of speaking and a habit of pursing her lips and nodding abruptly when she had expressed an opinion, as though the subject were now closed.

She was wonderfully easy to imitate, and I was just then discovering that I had a flair for ridicule, like my mother's but cruder, that could be turned at will on teachers and classmates. Apparently I was just as capable of unkindness as any of the other girls. In fact, I was particularly good at it. Just as I was discovering this talent in myself, an audience materialized. When I performed my Marjorie Martinelle routine for a few of the girls in the second-floor bathroom, they howled and collapsed on the tiles and sent out a scout to shout down the stairwell to summon more girls. I did it for them, too, and for others, and soon I was spending my recesses at the center of a gaggle of gossipers jammed into the rain shelter next to the swings. When I walked down Main Street after school I was at the center of a traveling, giggling human knot. We turned the corner at Spring Street and headed for the five-and-dime, where we pooled our allowance money and bought sacks full of candy. That year new kinds had appeared on the market, or at least newly packaged kinds. There were bright candy dots on strips of paper, bought by the yard, and envelopes of Lik-m-Aid, which stung sweetly when you poured it into your mouth and left an orange or green trench

running down the center of your tongue, and tiny wax bottles filled with sugar syrup. You ripped off the tops of these
with your teeth and knocked back the sixteenth of an ounce
contained within. One or another among us would carry a
partial pack of cigarettes (often it was my mother's Kents) to
pass around when we'd gotten away from the eyes of adults
and finished glutting ourselves with candy.

One day, as five or six of us were walking abreast along the
dirt road behind Spring Street, all of us laughing, we rounded
a corner and came upon Bob Bahnson, taking a shortcut on
his way back from classes. It had been some time since I'd
dropped by the Bahnsons' apartment and he did a double
take at the sight of me, rattling along happily in the midst of
a gang of girls. As we passed, he reached out a hand to tou-
sle my hair. Who was that? everyone demanded, their heads
swiveling, and I had the pleasure of seeing how impressed
they all were that I knew Caroline's husband.

Now I had fresh happiness to add to the account I had
been storing up from the episode in Jerry Panken's parents'
walk-in closet and from M. Rustin's Christmas pageant. I was
suddenly rich, but even so I found that I had little pity for my
solitary envious self of a few months earlier. My after-school
wanderings seemed pathetic to me now. Duncan McDougal
was an embarrassment and Tom Sommers was a worse one.
Even Eileen Mannion seemed not quite the thing anymore.

Everybody was constrained in her presence. More than once when I passed her in the hall, her eyes cast down and her smile private, I thought of the statue of the chilly little Virgin at the altar of the Catholic church. I dared to wonder whether Eileen hadn't really always been the creature of her family's expectations that she had recently become—if the death of Sandy had only served to bring out her true nature.

But my new happiness was fragile, absolutely contingent on my acceptance by the girls. It required maintenance. However exhausting and anxious the effort, I needed to work to keep myself at the solid center of the group; otherwise at any moment I might fall through its fringes into banishment. This meant that even though I knew that every repetition of my Marjorie Martinelle imitation brought me closer to the moment when the girls grew tired of it, I had to perform it on demand. When the group in the rain shelter caught sight of Marjorie plodding across the playground toward the swings, they all turned to me with glee in their eyes. "Do it," they commanded. "DO IT!" I stepped outside, where there was room to execute the carrying-milk-cans walk and did it, over and over again, in full view of its subject, who sat on the swing I had occupied for years of recesses—the pariah's swing—toeing the ground with her sneaker and pretending not to see.

When I questioned my own behavior, a fresh, stinging indignation rose up in me to justify it. How did Marjorie dare to be so self-satisfied in her ugliness? It was a culpable kind of thickheadedness, almost a moral failing. Did she imagine that people didn't notice? Like the patrolling scavenger fish that keeps the water free of organic debris, I had found a usefulness, a place in the scheme of things.

———

Bucky Watts," my mother had said to me once, "is a blob. You are, too, but you're a blob with wit and imagination." I don't remember what occasioned this remark; I'd probably been left out of some party at Bucky's house. I think my mother must have felt the sting of my exclusion herself: the Wattses were wealthy and unconnected to the college, pillars of Williamstown society. Some strong feeling must have motivated her to say something so uncharacteristically candid and tactless. I'm grateful now for that remark, as I am for any of the glimpses my mother gave me into the normally opaque workings of her mind.

At the time, though, her observation about Bucky and me hurt my feelings. I knew I was a blob, but it was hard to accept that my mother looked at me that way. I also knew that what was inner was more important than what was outer, but that was not much consolation. I took it on faith that I had wit and imagination, though these capacities were not fully subject to my will and located too far from the center of my personality to claim confidently as my own. In any case, they were quite useless to me in my life as a child, no help at all on the playground or in the classroom.

Bucky, as my mother pointed out, was dull as well as fat, and yet she had been powerful and popular from the third grade on. As it happened, that was the year when I began to understand how the social dynamics of Williamstown society were enacted in miniature on the playground at Pine Cobble. I realized that Bucky's popularity had something to do with the fact that she owned a horse, but I had never found that a sufficient explanation. It was only when I was lifted out of pariahdom that I came to understand the real basis for her popularity. She was a sergeant-at-arms figure, stolid and loyal, exerting a calming influence on the more volatile girls and preserving the group's traditions. She was also something of a pet.

I have no idea what became of Bucky, but I can speculate. I wouldn't be surprised if she lost weight after puberty and grew steadily more passable-looking through adolescence. And in spite of her dullness, she probably did fairly well in boarding school: her reputation for dependability and her activities in student government would carry the day with her teachers. No doubt she was the kind of girl who is held up to others as an example of the way that perspiration will often trump inspiration. I'll bet that during her last year in college, she was elected president of her class. I feel sure that life as an adult has been characterized by steadiness and slowly gathering success. I imagine that she spent her early adulthood burrowing deep into family and civic life in some leafy, affluent suburb, serving on the school board, active in the Junior League and, when her children were grown, chairing fund-raising drives for charities.

She would continue to ride, perhaps breed horses. These days she might well look something like that matron in tennis whites I noticed the other day, eating salad with a group of women in the shady courtyard of a restaurant here in Houston—the one who looked up briefly from under her visor as I walked by. Our eyes met for an instant. Then we lowered them quickly, like a pair of old enemies who have agreed not to acknowledge one another. I thought: *Here is a woman who can't remember a time when she hasn't been on the inside of things.* She was lean and well tended, almost handsome, if a little leathery, much evolved and improved since I last saw her in the sixth grade—if indeed this woman was Bucky, that is, which of course she wasn't.

In the years before my new popularity, Bucky was the only girl in the class I dared to hate. She returned the sentiment. The sneer on her doughy face carried a special message for me: *Yes, I'm stupid,* it said. *But even I know enough to hold* you *in contempt.* Once, in the girl's room, she caught me in the act of hiking up my tights; my back was turned, and I hadn't realized that the door to the stall had swung open. "I thought *I* was fat," she remarked, and the occupants of the two stalls flanking mine laughed. But now that she was the guarantor of my status as insider, the scornful envy I'd felt toward her changed overnight to shaky gratitude—to love, in fact. Good old Bucky! This was the way everyone felt, but I felt it with the ardor of a convert.

Four of the seven girls in that group are a blur in my memory now. The two I remember, aside from Bucky, were the power holders, the ones with the authority to admit or dismiss. One was Sue Dixon, whose distinction was her advanced state of sexual maturity: she had real breasts in sixth grade, not just puffed-out nipples, and she had started menstruating over the summer. The other was Dixie Wiggins, an amiable chipmunk of a girl, loved by everyone. These were the girls who drew me in.

Late in January, the annual John Jay ski movie was shown at Chapin Hall. This was an important event in Williamstown, second only to the yearly visit of the Budapest String Quartet. John Jay, a slender toothy man in green suspenders and a feathered Tyrolean hat, was a sort of Santa Claus figure to us in Williamstown, a costumed eccentric with one highly specialized function whose yearly visit was anticipated for months. He narrated the film, pacing the stage, his shadow rippling over the dancing images on the screen behind him. Scenes were shown of a skier's-eye-view of his progress down the slopes of mountains all over the world: Italy, Portugal, Austria, Peru. At the end of the evening he showed us what everyone had come to see, the footage shot in the Berkshires. We all roared when we recognized the gift shop at the bottom of the hairpin turn on the Mohawk Trail, the one that had to be rebuilt twice because trucks whose brakes had failed rammed into it. We laughed when John Jay was shown mugging in front of the familiar blue and yellow Dutch Hill sign, cheered when he toasted us with a German beer stein as he sat by the fire in the lodge.

The hall, as always, was packed for this event. The year before I had stood in back by the door, my view of the screen obstructed by the heads and torsos of Williams students, but this year I was seated between Sue and Dixie and directly in front of Bucky, right up against the railing on the balcony. We all four drew in our breath as John Jay began his rattling progress down a ski jump ramp, snow sparkling prismatically on the lens of the shuddering camera strapped to his chest. We all four gasped as he soared into an arc of unsupported glory. For a long, thrilling moment, the camera tilted upward and lost sight of the slope altogether—even of the tips of John Jay's orange skis. We saw nothing but our familiar dusky mountains bouncing and trembling against an implacably blue expanse of sky.

Lilac Time

My father returned from one of his New York stays early that spring and announced that we were leaving Williamstown. He had decided to resign from Williams and accept a full-time position at the Ford Foundation. He had already made arrangements to rent an apartment for us on Riverside Drive. Before Labor Day we would pack up our furniture and belongings, give the white wedding-cake house back to the college, and move to New York.

My mother wept, but my eyes stayed dry. I was disconcerted to find that I was not as sad as I might have expected to be. What I felt was quite supportable and suspiciously pleasant: melancholy, not grief. The fact was that I was excited at the news about New York. Already, the scenes of my child-hood had shrunk back a little into their frames. I loved Williamstown, but I was also eager to leave it, if only because then I could begin my lifelong project of remembering it.

—

In fifth grade, the boys had been fixated on breasts, but by the second semester of sixth we were all, boys and girls alike, obsessed with every aspect of sex. This was the era of com-plicated and lamely premised jokes about Grandma Moses's Whore House and the Old Log Inn and Johnny Fuckerfaster. We had been segregating ourselves by gender on the play-ground since fourth grade, but now the centrifugal action of Eros had integrated us completely. We assembled to tell these jokes whenever we were out of the hearing of adults—not only to titillate ourselves, but also to exchange informa-tion about sexual intercourse. Most of us had a grasp of basic anatomy and at least a partial vocabulary, but there were large gaps in our understanding. (I, for one, could not have located my clitoris, even if I'd known I had one.) These jokes offered answers, however distorted and inaccurate, to ques-tions about sexual mechanics that all of us would have been embarrassed to ask openly. For me they also opened up a larger question: when we attained sexual maturity, would we find ourselves living in the world of dirty jokes? I pictured this as a desolate place, a land of leers and low contrivances, where sex was the only reality and all the accoutrements of life—rooms, books, furniture, food, etc.—were reduced to the status of props. I saw a doorway off some narrow cobbled lane where men with painfully swollen genitals lined up to be serviced by an obliging widow.

And were the adults we knew even now watching for a chance to get behind our backs to copulate? Was this on their minds all the time? Could we assume that every one of them was subject to the jackrabbit sexual avidity of the protagonists of dirty jokes? Could this be true, for example, of Mr. Allen and Mr. Cartwright, the two elderly bachelors who lived in furnished rooms on Southworth Street, whose constitutional took them past the Williams Inn every day, and who stopped to ask after my parents and my brother and sister and consoled me when James died? Was the school principal in his office right now with the door closed, going at it on the floor with Mrs. McGraw, the volunteer secretary, whose daughter Alice was in fourth grade and whose son David was in first? These were absurd questions. I knew that, and I asked them in order to reassure myself. But then I thought of the photograph Duncan, Tom, and I had found under the bleachers. I thought of Dodson Odetts prancing around on the flatbed truck at football rallies, wriggling into an imaginary girdle.

I thought of Simon Lavin, the gangly redheaded Englishman with an outsize Adam's apple, who had recently hired as the new boys' soccer coach. That spring he developed the habit of wandering over to the playing field where Caroline Bahnson supervised the girls. While the boys ran laps and the girls executed deep knee bends, Caroline and Simon—we were allowed to call them both by their first names—stood on the sidelines together smoking and talking. Once we saw them share a cigarette, and on another occasion I noticed Simon extracting Caroline's from between her fingers and applying its burning tip to his own. I drew Dixie Wiggins's attention to this, and soon all the girls were whispering.

What was it about them that was so disturbing and so fascinating? Was it that they stood a fraction of an inch too close to one another? Was it also that Simon was so tall and knobby, while Caroline was so short and busty? Was it that the juxtaposition of their bodies sent an ancient message of convexity and concavity? Surely there was something unmistakable going on between these two, something oblique and implicit, something lacking in the uncomplicated frontal happiness that Caroline and Bob showed the world. Or was there?

—

That was the spring I fell from grace, but before I fell from grace I fell in love, first with Bob Bahnson and then—having recognized the need to make a midcourse correction—with his noble and chivalrous love for his wife. I had the opportunity to fall in love this way because for the first time I was included in the cast of the annual school play. This was a musical about a town that burned down and was rebuilt in a day by its determined inhabitants. It involved a lot of choral singing and marching back and forth across the stage carrying ladders and hammers and saws. I've long since forgotten its title, but I remember that I wore a floor-length carpenter's apron and a cardboard ruler behind one ear, and I also remember an exhilarating smell of freshly cut plywood when the stage set, a waist-high cityscape, was itself under construction.

The faculty-wife faction at Pine Cobble must have been instrumental in the choice of this play, with its many crowd scenes and wholesome communitarian theme. It was a sign that the administration had taken note of my new social status that I was given a small speaking part. This consisted of one line: "Let's build a brand-new town!" My role required me to break free of a milling crowd of laborers, rush forward to the front of the stage, fling out my arms, and declaim it. Simple enough, but I bungled it in every possible way, starting by blurting out my line before I'd gotten halfway across the stage. Art Siegenthal, the director, broke me of that, but then I couldn't get the hang of shouting it out over the heads of an imaginary audience. Instead, I scanned the room anxiously for a pair of eyes to meet. More often than not I forgot to throw my arms out, or did it so stiffly that I heard titters from the assembled masons and bricklayers behind me. Caroline Bahnson pulled me aside after rehearsal one day and told me that she and Bob would need to help me work on my voice.

The Bahnsons no longer lived at the end of Spring Street. They'd moved into a building not far from Pine Cobble, a neglected Georgian mansion the college had recently acquired and divided into apartments for married graduate students and young faculty. I reached it by cutting around the skating pond and ducking under a barbed-wire fence and squeezing through a line of evergreens. It was early April when I first visited there, one of those skittery spring days, sunny and cloudy, with an occasional icy breeze. Pink and white crocuses poked up through muddy pebbles. I climbed three flights of dusty stairs and walked down a broad carpeted hallway where bicycles and baby carriages were parked. I smelled onions cooking, heard someone practicing a Chopin étude I recognized from my sister's days as a piano student.

As it happened, Caroline was not at home. Bob answered the door and led me into the new apartment, which consisted of three boxy unfurnished rooms and an expanse of splintery parquet floor. Bob had been painting; dropcloths were laid down and every window was propped open. Books—apparently from Bob's carrel in the basement of the library; there had been none in the old apartment—had been stacked in piles along one wall.

There was a sense of bohemian freedom in the dusty, echoing emptiness of these rooms, with their high ceilings and pastry-cream moldings. I found it so exhilarating that I had to stop myself from skipping and twirling. The conviction suddenly came to me that one day when I was grown I would move into an apartment very much like this—in Greenwich Village, perhaps, or Paris. There would be a view, and a balcony overlooking a courtyard. I would move from one freedom to another. As Bob showed me around—how flattering it was to be treated like an equal!—I got a quick glimpse through an open door at the Bahnsons' bed, a box-spring and mattress on the floor. It was left unmade, a blanket thrown over it unevenly. I'd never seen a bed positioned like that before, dead center in the middle of the floor. Evidently the Bahnsons had placed it there deliberately, so that they could see the night sky through all four windows as they lay in bed together. Looking at the bed, I thought of a broken-spined book lying open.

Bob moved the ladder over in front of the living room's bay window and directed me to stand on the middle rung. He placed himself at the other end of the room and cupped an ear. "Let's build a brand-new town!" I called out. He cupped his ear again. "Let's build a brand-new town!" I bellowed. Bob gestured me down from the ladder. He stood behind me, took my hand and pressed it against my ribs at the center of my chest, just below my heart. I struggled not to giggle, and failed. Bob ignored it. "That's your diaphragm," he said. "Try to move your voice from your throat down to your chest. Just say the line. Don't shout."

"Let's build a brand-new town." Even though my voice quavered, I could feel its authority; in my own ears it sounded newly adult. "Good," said Bob. "Much better. You practice that at home." He moved away toward the kitchen and I followed; apparently the lesson was over. At the door he squatted and squeezed my shoulders. All the way down the stairs I continued to feel the weight and warmth of his hands.

———

Early May came, and lilac time began. The plump white ones appeared first, then the violet and, last, the deep purple double-blossomed narrow ones, shaped like pinecones. Every spring there came a warm windy day when the colonization was complete and the whole town reeked sweetly. Everyone walking out into the morning inhaled, closed their eyes, stood still. For the two or three weeks they lasted, the lilacs were so plentiful and their rubbery scent so pervasive that it was as if some new currency had swamped the local aesthetic economy. They bobbed and rustled around us like heavenly emissaries, whispering rumors of a land where there was no such thing as scarcity. Children tore off branches—you couldn't wrest them free of the bush without peeling the bark in long strips—and carried great careless armloads home to their mothers, who never thought to scold them. After two or three weeks, the blossoms began to rust; after another they shriveled. I could hardly bear to look at them. We were let out of school early during those last weeks. The understanding was that we were to use the time to study for exams, but Sue and Dixie and Bucky and I ran and skipped down the hill to Spring Street to buy penny candy. Or rather, they ran and skipped and I walked and trotted a few yards behind them, laboring to keep up.

Later we watched *American Bandstand* in Dixie's pink and green bedroom. We clustered around her tightly as she lay on her back on her canopied bed, a marvelous little TV balanced on her stomach, mesmerized by the camera's tour of willfully slack teenaged faces. We watched as it zoomed in over some boy's oscillating shoulder to consider a dark sideburn growing low on the cheek of an otherwise pretty girl, a jaw working a wad of gum, the enlarged pores of an oily nose. When the camera panned up and away to show the dancers lining up to do the Stroll, we scrambled off the bed and shuffled across the carpet in our stocking feet to the beat of that hypnotically sinister dirge. Then came the opening credits of *The Edge of Night* and we turned the TV off and got down to the real business of the afternoon, our ongoing discussion of Caroline and Simon.

Every day we found some new morsel to chew on. Sometimes it was a gesture we'd noticed during field hockey practice after lunch that day. Caroline might have leaned over to murmur something to Simon, or wrapped a strand of hair around one finger, or laughed a little too brightly. We set up dramatic scenes, the other girls taking turns at playing Caroline while I took the role of Simon, doing my best to imitate his bug-eyed poker face and twitching mouth. But perhaps Simon and Caroline had stayed apart that day. We found meaning even in their separations, which we interpreted in different ways depending on circumstances. If Mrs. Fritts had been out on one of her walkabouts, we took Simon's failure to slouch over to the girls' field and take his usual place next to Caroline to be a sign of his consciousness of guilt. If he simply kept his distance, and there was nothing to explain it, we posited a quarrel, or—more appealingly—a mutual renunciation.

What if Caroline was pregnant? I offered this one afternoon. The idea was a hit; we all fell into a frenzy, staggering around the room with our pelvises thrown out, supporting phantom bellies with our cupped hands. Dixie stuffed a pillow under her shirt and lay on the floor with her knees splayed, as if far gone in labor. Sue and Bucky knelt over her as she groaned, acting the part of nurse and midwife. I found myself pushed back a little, looking down over their shoulders. Even in those days of relative popularity I never for a moment felt I had penetrated the heart of the group. When everyone laughed I laughed, too, but there were moments when I felt the glee harden on my face like a glaze.

Pregnant by Bob? By Simon? By both? Could a woman be impregnated by more than one man? Bucky was pretty sure horses could, and cats. Sue thought not. We moved on to a general discussion of obstetrical anomalies. Sue's brother was born with a caul over his head. My mother spent six months in bed after my brother was born to prevent a clot in one of her legs from working loose and traveling to her heart and killing her. The vet stuck his arm all the way to his shoulder up one of the Wattses' mares to turn around a stuck foal. Dixie's aunt had given birth to a thing that looked like a baby at first but was really only a bag of skin full of hair and teeth.

—

School ended. I learned that I'd failed French, Math, and also, if I remember correctly, Geography. This was hardly surprising: I'd been failing for years. What was new was that I had barely passed English. What was also new, I realized with a start, was that I would be going to a new school next fall. At Pine Cobble I'd been promoted every year out of concern for my mother's feelings, but there was no reason to assume that this would happen in New York. And how would they know, looking at my grades, that I was actually very bright?

Actually very bright. This had been said about me so many times that I heard it as a hyphenated phrase: actually-very-bright. But *was* I actually very bright? This question had been hovering in the back of my mind as a prearticulate blur ever since the days when I watched Russell Barnes assemble jumbo jigsaw puzzles with the picture sides turned down, all without rising from a squat. Now I forced the thought into words: Could it be that I actually wasn't very bright? That I was simply stupid? But no, I knew I wasn't dull all the way through like Bucky.

Was I—here I struggled to find a way to conceive of this paradoxical idea—was I *falsely* bright? I searched for analogies from the natural world: perhaps I was like one of those camouflage creatures I'd seen in Walt Disney nature movies: insects that looked like sticks, fish that puffed themselves up to intimidate predators. Was my facility with words only the mental equivalent of this kind of adaptive disguise?

My real fear was that in New York they'd send me to another tester, more sophisticated than the man in North Adams with the argyle socks, and that this time they'd find whatever it was my mother and the doctors had been looking for. I imagined a team of white-coated researchers ushering me into a room like an operating theater, but dim. I would be told to lie down on a high padded table. A great shining machine would slowly descend from the ceiling until it hung a fraction of an inch above my eyes. It would aim a narrow

beam of light into my brain and the clipboard-carrying pro-
fessionals would gather around to measure just how bright I
really was.

—

When I wasn't gossiping with Sue and Dixie and Bucky, I
spent the days of late May and early June walking and riding
my bike around Williamstown alone, saying good-bye. I paid
a visit to the Williams Inn lobby and lounge. Surprise balls
were still on sale in the gift shop, but the chocolate mints on
which I used to spend my allowance had been replaced by
individually wrapped hard candies. A line of alums in
madras jackets sat at the bar, but there were no fond smiles
as I walked by. I'd long since reached the age of invisibility.

I followed the old paths through the Williams Inn gardens.
Good-bye, I said to the graveled walkways and the henhouse
and the ranks of red and yellow tulips—actually said it aloud.
I said good-bye to the Williams Inn annex where Mrs.
Thorn lived—she had moved away several years before—
and to the Barneses' house. I sat on the lip of Library Hill
and at the foot of the Haystack Monument, rehearsing my
memories and ventilating my anxieties about moving to
New York. I knew my recent popularity would not be trans-
ferable, but I was reconciled to that. Being popular was a
strain, and it would be better to leave before I was dropped.

Are You Happy?

I visited the basement of Lehman Hall, which somebody had made an effort to clean up—the mattresses had been stacked and pushed into a corner and the place smelled of disinfectant—and the frog pond and the wild woods behind the Williams tennis courts, where James had once hared off after a squirrel and I wandered for hours calling him. Good-bye. I wobbled my bike to a stop on pebbled roads to gaze out over the scenes of my years with Duncan and Tom: Indian Country and New Inverness and the roads we walked when we sneaked out of our houses at night. Good-bye again.

Good-bye to the freshman quad and the student union and the pool tables and radio station in its basement. Good-bye to the viewing room and the damaged tiles in its ceiling. Good-bye to the skirted pine in front of the McDougals' house and the Women's Exchange and the train station. Good-bye to the dowdy houses on Southworth Street and to Mrs. Imhoff's nursery school. Good-bye to the skating pond and the cliffs behind Spring Street and the rink. Good-bye to the House of Walsh. Good-bye to the infirmary and to the little museum in the biology building and to Chapin Hall and the Terror. Good-bye to the shadow-streaked territories under the bleachers at the football field, where surprises could reliably be found. Good-bye to packs of roaming dogs. Good-bye to the pool at Sand Springs and the glowing bottles ranked on shelves in the warehouse. Good-bye to wild strawberries. Good-bye to black-eyed Susans and Queen

Anne's lace. Good-bye to the dying elms. I climbed Stone Hill and sat at the top of the trail in the stone chair, looking down on a high meadow through a line of birches, their silver leaves fluttering. Good-bye, Williamstown.

This was only the first of several farewell tours I took before we moved away in August. I found these extended leave-takings endlessly comforting, and the quiet old town, deep in summer green, endured them patiently. My good-byes were far from final; I continue to say them again whenever I return to Williamstown, and nearly every night when I go to sleep.

What kind of unnatural child was I, always pushing now into then? What kind of unnatural adult have I become, always writing elegies in my head? Other children, with their narrow, darting shadows, lived in the present, but I lagged a fraction of an instant behind the action, waiting for the blurred surface of the present moment to settle and resolve into the clarity of the past. By the time we left Williamstown for New York I was just becoming conscious of this almost imperceptible hesitation and the way it seemed to set me apart. Perhaps it was the thing that had made me different all along. Other children must have registered it unconsciously, in the part of their brains that neurologists identify with our reptilian heritage. My eulogizing impulse kept me slightly but definitively out of sync with the world that moved around me when I was a child, and has continued to do so ever since.

Are You Happy?

Once, some years after my father's death, I visited my mother in Williamstown. I hadn't seen her since the funeral. She was still living in the house they'd planned to retire to, the one with the view of the mountains and the catalpa tree under which my husband and I had been married. She was drinking hard and steadily now, two eight-ounce martinis before dinner, half a bottle of wine with the meal. I kept pace with her easily: I weighed half again what she did and my capacity for alcohol was formidable. I think she was grateful for this; it was something neither my brother nor my sister would do. After dinner she excused herself to perform her periodontal routine and take her bath. She returned in her bathrobe and slippers, releasing the scent of Yardley Red Roses talcum powder with every step. She poured us both snifters of brandy. We each lit a final cigarette. Things had been tense during the afternoon and earlier in the evening, but now we sat in a glow of alcoholic fellowship.

Then she excused herself and climbed, a little unsteadily, up the stairs to her bedroom. When she reached the landing, she turned to look down at me with a tender smile. "Try to be happy, Em," she said, and disappeared down the darkened hallway.

I've wondered at that remark ever since. Try to be happy? What did she mean by that? Was it a simple benediction, or did it carry an implicit apology? Was it a kind of rueful countermanding of the message she had given me in Williams-town when we sang songs at the piano together, when we took walks to admire the new moon?

Try to be happy? *Now you tell me?*

—

I spent those last months in Williamstown reading *Le Morte D'Arthur*. Bob Bahnson had become a knightly figure in my imagination, an embodiment of chaste, high-minded, vulner-able masculinity. As a result, my love for him had changed; now I was less in love with him than I was in love with his wounded love for Caroline. I had never quite dared to imag-ine touching or kissing him. He was a vital, hairy adult male and in truth I was a little afraid of him.

I was also, more generally, drunk on love—on the *idea* of love. When I saw young couples walking together that sum-mer on the campus at dusk I was filled with admiration and pity. They were not only more beautiful than other people; they were more important. All the latent romance of a lovely summer evening gathered around them in a nimbus, and that particular evening became continuous with all the summer evenings that had ever come and gone. They were like the kamikaze pilots I'd seen in newsreels at the Walden Theatre, living among us like heroes, soon to be ghosts.

Are You Happy?

Sue and Dixie and Bucky and I were united in our Manichaean attitude toward sex and love. Sex was gross, fantastic, comical. Love was ennobling and inherently tragic. Reluctantly, we allowed that everyone had genitals and sexual urges—disgusting as we found the thought, especially as it applied to our parents—but we reserved love for people of roughly college age. Sexual desirability was a qualifying condition, but sexual union was not love's aim. Sexual attraction pervaded love, but we required it to take a highly attenuated form. Like the medieval chroniclers of courtly love, we understood love to be unstable, not a fit foundation for marriage. Love was inimical to marriage and could enter into it only retrospectively, through the portal created by loss. Adultery was the only fully sexualized form of love that we could stomach.

Do you think he knows? Dixie asked. She meant Bob, with whom all of us sympathized passionately. Yes, I answered, I think he probably does. What if he came home and found them? He would be very very angry and hurt, I said, but I think he would let her decide what to do, whether to stay or leave. What I can't remember is whether or not I even tried to pretend—to myself—that I believed that Simon and Caroline were having an affair. I think I kept the matter a blur in my mind. I knew that I had to keep the suspicion alive so that I could continue to be the keeper of the

Bahnson story, so that all eyes would turn to me, so that I could go on feeling the proprietary warmth that spread in my chest whenever I had occasion to speak Bob's name.

Someone—probably it was me—suggested that we had a responsibility to tell Bob what we knew. Means were discussed: an anonymous note left in his library carrel? No, came the consensus. That could be taken as a prank. It was here that I either volunteered or was pressed into volunteering to be the carrier of the news.

An opportunity soon presented itself. Late one afternoon I looked out my bedroom window and saw my father and Bob emerge from Fernald Hall together and cross College Place. They were deep in talk; evidently they intended to continue the discussion in his study. I came down the stairs and stationed myself by the front window to watch them as they approached. They were a study in contrasting types, my father long-faced, balding, saturnine, Bob chunky and burly, with a loud delighted laugh. The two of them were deep in discussion when they came in the door. They continued as they walked down the hall—without noticing me—and climbed the stairs to my father's study, where they spent the next hour going over my father's comments on an article that Bob hoped to submit to a professional journal.

When the door finally opened, releasing a swirl of pipe smoke into the hall where I'd been loitering and waiting for my father's voice to rise to a tone of dismissal, I found I had to wait still longer. Just as Bob started down the hall, raising his eyebrows and smiling at me, my father leaned out the study door and called him back. My father propped himself against the doorjamb, sucking at his infuriating pipe, taking his measured, thoughtful time. I can't begin to characterize their conversation: academic shoptalk had as much meaning to me as the shrieks of a tropical bird. I did take note, though, of my father's invitation to Bob to drop off another draft of his paper at the department. He'd take it along and read it on the train, he said. He'd be at Bob's disposal to talk again in a few weeks. "That'd be such a help," said Bob. "You betcha," said my father.

Bob was released. I stepped out of the shadows and placed myself in his path. He threw out his hands in delighted welcome; I could see that his talk with my father had left him elated. "I have something to tell you," I said. "Oh?" said Bob. Just then, my mother appeared at the end of the hall. "Bob," she called out. "How is Caroline?" "She's doing just fine," Bob said, raising a hand to stay my request and turning to smile in my mother's direction.

"Please be sure and give her our best," said my mother. She went on to add that she'd been wondering whether the two of them might be able to use one of the couches in the family room, the wooden one with foam cushions. She wished she could say it was in pristine condition. Perhaps he'd like to take a look.

—

By late June the rustling hush of full summer had settled in around us. My mother was deep in packing, and both of the living rooms were full of boxes and echoes. I was teaching myself to drink coffee, mixed with milk, and working hard on my smoking. Every day I pocketed handfuls of my mother's Kents, knowing she was too preoccupied to keep track of them.

She was packing books one day, loading them into two sets of boxes, some destined for the New York apartment and others to be carted off in the Plymouth to the Women's Exchange. I was expected to help, but I was distracted by a book I found on an upper shelf. This was *A Dog's Head* by Jean Dutourd. On the dust jacket there was, sure enough, a donnishly dressed man, pipe in hand, with a spaniel's head. I'd discovered this book years earlier, and looked through it curiously, but then it disappeared: I'm sure my mother considered it inappropriate for children. It was a kind of fable, translated from the French. Somewhere in the middle, I remembered, the dog-headed man found a woman willing to love him. He and this woman—here I'm paraphrasing—"kept no secrets from one another about their bodies." This passage had left a deep impression on me, and when I put my hand on the book I took it up with me to the secret room at the head of the back stairs and leafed through the pages, trying to find it.

Then the door opened and my mother was there. I can reconstruct now what she must have seen. It was twelve-year-old me, lying on the floor wrapped in an army blanket, a smutty novel in my hand, surrounded by piles of books that had disappeared from the shelves over the years, and by cups of cold coffee stuffed with doused butts.

She was speechless with anger. This was the first of two times I saw her this way. The other was twenty years later, just before my father's funeral. She and my sister and I were sorting through his clothes in the walk-in closet adjacent to his study in the Wyoming Avenue town house. I wandered away, as I tend to do when people are working, and when I turned to come back she was there before me in the hallway, very thin, with hands that shook in a palsy of rage. She hissed at me that I was no help, that I should get out, just go.

—

Bob returned to talk to my father. This time the consultation was brief; my father had to excuse himself to pack for another New York trip. While the two of them shook hands warmly at the door to my father's study, I ducked down the stairs and waited for Bob at the front door.

Once again he squatted—hardly necessary, now that I had grown tall enough to reach his nose—and rested his hands on my shoulders, a fond, level amusement in his eyes. I looked down, nervously, at his bulging khaki thighs. "What's this about, Emily?"

"Caroline," I whispered. A flicker of surprise passed over his face, then confusion. I could see a scene change in progress behind his eyes. The gratifying interval in my father's study was being hauled away, leaving the stage momentarily empty. "Caroline?"

"Caroline and *Simon*."

He was truly puzzled. I wondered for a moment whether he even knew who Simon was. I waited. Still more incomprehension. A baffled, radiant smile. His face was so close to mine that I could see the pulse working in his throat, the saliva glistening on his teeth. It seemed to me that an awful hum and glow was beginning to emanate from his person, even as his eyes shone with simple kindness. I found I had to resist the temptation to work my shoulders loose from his hands and back away. But then I saw that the dime had dropped. The long moment ended. "I'll tell you what," he said, slowly rising to a standing position. "Why don't you drop by the apartment next Saturday around two. We can talk about it."

—

During one of our last weeks in Williamstown, on the way to some errand, my mother took an abrupt detour. She pulled the Plymouth to a stop directly opposite the spot on the banks of the Green River where she used to gather watercress. The river was wide and shallow there, lined with flat rocks. A great willow tree overhung the bank. As we sat in the car looking out, three or four black and white cows came shambling down to the river's edge and lowered their great wedge-shaped heads to drink. My mother lit a cigarette jerkily and turned her face away. Her shoulders began to shake.

This was the moment when the balance between us shifted. Sitting there next to my weeping mother, my face averted, I understood that of the two of us I was the stronger organism. My appetite for experience was larger, my ability to metabolize it more robust. I had always understood the old business of mourning the past as a kind of game I played with my mother, a game for which I had a particular aptitude. Soon it would become a vocation for me, later a profession. It was no game for my mother; she wept in earnest.

—

The myth I've lived with all my life was that my happiness was lost when we left Williamstown. This wasn't true, of course; it would have gone if we'd stayed. In fact it had been dribbling away for years, like sand from a leaky pocket, and what remained had come pouring out at the moment when

I said "Caroline and Simon." It was as if I had plunged my hand into the pocket and ripped the fabric wide open. After that, it was inevitable that Bob and Caroline would put together the story I had invented and it was inevitable—being the people they were—that they would do what they did.

When the time came, I followed Bob through the long narrow kitchen into the living room, where my instinct that I'd walked into a setup was confirmed. Caroline was there, of course, on the sofa, her knees drawn up to her chest. She was wearing heavy oatmeal-colored kneesocks and beaded moccasins. On her face was a complex but instantly readable expression of fond disappointment. I looked around and saw the mercy of this. There was nothing bohemian about the place now; it had been thoroughly domesticated. I recognized rugs from the old apartment at the end of Spring Street. The Bahnsons had bought a coffee table; family pictures in silver frames sat on the mantel; muslin curtains hung in the windows. A crocheted afghan was folded over the far arm of the couch. The whole room was Caroline's. I glanced into the bedroom and saw that the bed had been pushed back against a wall and tidily made. Bob was her husband, and she *was* pregnant, of course. My mother already knew: that was why she had made a point of asking after Caroline.

Bob sat down next to Caroline. Together, in a motion so smoothly coordinated that it might have been choreographed in advance, they leaned forward and extended their arms to me. For a moment I could only stare at them, stunned. But no mind stays baffled for long; a system of branching intuitions sprang up instantly, conveying meaning across the breach.

I understood that Caroline and Bob had decided to bypass blame and proceed directly to love and pity. I was able to recognize this tactic because it was of a piece with the gentle reforms the faculty wives had been making at my school. A harsh scolding would have been the only astringent strong enough to dissolve my humiliation, but the Bahnsons had decided to deny me that. They offered another kind of comfort, and to receive it I had only to walk into their outstretched arms. But I found I couldn't.

I hated the Bahnsons for their loving trickery and their smug pride in their own enlightenment. They were lost to me, and so, I realized at that moment, was my happiness. Their intervention offered me no hope or help, only a diagnosis of my condition. I took a step backward, but I was no more capable of flight than I was of speech. Bob's expression was imploring, Caroline's a tender moue of concern. They held their positions like a *tableau vivant* while I stood in a dazzle of shame.

———

Late in August my father loaded the Plymouth and we made the move to New York. We set off in the morning and drove past meadows full of goldenrod and Indian paintbrush. We saw the last of our Berkshire Mountains, dark blue and coolly remote at this time of year. My mother wore sunglasses and wept quietly; I could see her lower lip tremble as she looked out the window. Once again my eyes stayed dry.

My brother and I started squabbling almost immediately. Kicks were exchanged. By the time we reached Hancock my father had had enough. He pulled the car over and rearranged the luggage so that we were separated by a suitcase. I was happy enough to be confined this way, wedged up against the car window. I had begun to cherish privacy and on this occasion I needed it in order to register my reactions. With every mile I felt more free. I kept a talismanic picture of Manhattan in my mind, a late-afternoon view of gold and charcoal rooftops and terraces I saw once from the window of an Upper West Side apartment bathroom. The simple and liberating fact was that in New York nobody would know me. Whatever bad things might happen, I would have another chance.

On the Saw Mill River Parkway my father had discovered rest areas where you could buy cups of quite palatable chicken soup from a vending machine. We stopped at one of these. My mother had composed herself by now, but she declined the soup. My father advised us to use the bathrooms in the stone shelter and to take the opportunity to stretch our legs. Carrying my paper cone of lukewarm broth, I wandered out to the manicured swath of grass by the highway. As the cars swished past I drank it. My father was right: it was very salty and ineffably delicious.

Back in the car, my father's mood had turned cheerful and expansive. He consulted his watch and announced that in less than an hour and a half, Andy and I would be exploring the apartment. I had learned how to be sullen by now, and I stifled my impulse to ask questions about my new room—how big it was, how many windows it had, and what I would see when I looked out of them. Instead, I summoned up the gold and charcoal rooftops once again, keeping the image steadily before my mind's eye as we traveled along the Henry Hudson Parkway and into the city. Let history begin.

ACKNOWLEDGMENTS

Thanks to Elyse Cheney, my loyal and skillful agent, and thanks to Julie Grau, my editor, whose tactful intelligence has helped me enormously. Thanks most of all to George Sher, my husband, first reader, and most exacting critic.

ABOUT THE AUTHOR

Emily Fox Gordon is an award-winning essayist and the author of the memoir *Mockingbird Years: A Life In and Out of Therapy*, a *New York Times* Notable Book. Her work has appeared in *American Scholar; Time; Pushcart Prize Anthology XXIII,* and *XXIX; Anchor Essay Annual; The New York Times Book Review; Boulevard;* and *Salmagundi*. She has taught at Rice University and the University of Wyoming, and lives in Houston.